LIVING WITH
STRESS

LIVING WITH
STRESS

Biblical Truths to Manage Your Life

CHARLES R. GERBER

COLLEGE PRESS ✪ PUBLISHING CO

Joplin, Missouri

Cover Design: Mark A. Cole

International Standard Book Number 0-89900-852-6

CONTENTS

INTRODUCTION

Readers of my books often comment favorably on the way I have integrated Scripture with psychology through my writings; however, my writing is not designed to do that. I do not want to integrate Scripture with psychology; instead, it is my goal to put Scripture where it rightfully belongs, elevated far above psychology.

As you read this study on stress, you will see that I frequently refer to the book of Psalms. This book could easily have been called *A "Stressful" Look at the Book of Psalms*. The following acrostic both defines the Psalms and offers clues to successful ways of dealing with our emotions and the stress which often accompanies them:

Praise
Song
Announcing the
Lord's
Message

More than any other book of the Bible, Psalms deals with emotions: grief, guilt, fear, anxiety, and dread. I am convinced that you can read any of the 150 chapters and find your emotions mirrored there. Psalms is the book of expressed emotion. I am also convinced that your life will be blessed if you read the psalms along with this study and let this wonderful book of the Bible minister to you. Fall in love with the Psalms; you will be blessed by them.

While stress is an inevitable and even necessary part of normal life, how important is it to keep stress at a manageable level? The answer to that depends upon how important your health is to you. If you value good health, you will want to listen to James Blumenthal, a professor in medical psychology at Duke University Medical Center: "In addition to diet, quitting smoking, and controlling blood pressure, you need to think about managing stress" to help avert potentially fatal heart problems. The October 27, 1997, American Medical Association's Archives of Internal Medicine gave results of Blumenthal's research on stress management, showing that there was a 75% reduction in risk of second heart attack or need for surgery in heart patients when stress was managed correctly.

As I conclude this introduction, I especially want to thank Dr. Daryl Morrical and his wife Linda for the countless number of times they have talked with me about the medical implications of stress on the physical body. Without their assistance, this project would not be as thorough as it is.

Chapter 1
WHAT IS STRESS?

No one in our time seriously questions the need for a book on handling stress. Quite obviously, stress is at epidemic proportions in the world, especially in the Western world. The worldwide web confirms this when it reports these three things: 1) Two-thirds of all visits to doctors are stress-related. 2) Medical costs attributed to stress are over one billion dollars a year. 3) Stress costs businesses one hundred fifty billion dollars a year in health insurance payouts, absenteeism, burnout, lost productivity, poor morale, and worker turnover.

Maureen S. Mulvaney, author of several books on stress, states, "Stress is killing us. Ninety-five percent of all illnesses are due to stress — the stresses of our lives, our jobs, our families." While some experts believe that abnormal stress is a contributing factor in 75% of all illnesses, Mulvaney's estimate of 95% makes that look conservative.

From these statistics you might conclude that we should get rid of all stress, but this would be wrong. We need a certain amount of stress to motivate us to live fully. Dr. Hans Selye, a researcher on stress, says, "Complete freedom from stress is death" (Jay Braun and Darwyn E. Linder, *Psychology Today*

[New York: Random House, 1979], p. 343). The opposite of stress is boredom, and prisoners in solitary confinement can testify to the truth of Selye's statement.

Selye and Laurence Cherry state further that good stress is actually beneficial; they call it "eustress," utilizing the Greek word *eu* for "good." They suggest that "Our aim should not be to completely avoid stress, which at any rate would be impossible, but to learn how to recognize our typical response to stress and then to try to modulate our lives in accordance with it." (From Hans Selye and Laurence Cherry, "On the Real Benefits of Eustress," *Psychology Today Magazine* [March 1978], p. 60.)

What Is Stress?

What is stress? G.L. Engel defines it this way: "Psychological stress refers to all processes, whether originating in the external environment or within the person, which impose a demand or requirement upon the organism [person] the resolution or handling of which requires . . . activity of the mental apparatus before any other system is involved or activated" (Karl Menninger, M.D., *The Vital Balance* [New York: The Viking Press, 1963], p. 129).

Selye writes:

> Stress is the body's non-specific response to any demand placed on it, whether that demand is pleasant or not. Sitting in a dentist chair is stressful, but so is enjoying a passionate kiss with a lover – after all, your pulse races, your breath quickens, your heartbeat soars. And yet who would forego such a pleasurable pastime simply because of the stress involved.
> (From Hans Selye and Laurence Cherry, "Benefits of Eustress," p. 60.)

I prefer a simpler definition to the two given above. Stress is defined in *Webster's Dictionary* as a "force that strains or deforms, mental or physical tension, urgency, pressure." It comes from the Old French word *estrecier*, a derivative from the Latin *strictus*, meaning to be drawn tight, compress, narrow. When a person undergoes stress, the options available to deal with it appear to be constricted, narrowed.

It is interesting to note that the word "stress" is not found in Scripture; however, the word "distress" is found 84 times in the NIV, and the word "distressed" is found 24 times. I conclude therefore, that stress is very much a biblical issue. The Bible deals not only with the causes and symptoms of stress but also the solutions.

Stress is a very unique response because it can come from the past, present, or future. When it comes from the past, it is frequently called depression or guilt. When it comes from the present, it is called burnout. When it comes from the future, it is called fear and anxiety.

We can recall men and women in the Bible who illustrate each of the above concepts. Haunted by his past, Jacob experienced guilt for having deceived Isaac, burnout when he confronted Laban's refusal to pay him, and fear when he was going to meet Esau (Gen. 32:7-8; 35:3). Eli had to deal with his past of raising undisciplined sons (1 Sam. 3:13) and suffered guilt over their wickedness. King Saul was filled with fear at the sound of Samuel's voice (1 Sam. 28:15). Elijah illustrates burnout in his cry that he is alone in his faith (1 Kings 19:1-18).

Meditating on the lives of these and many other men and women in the Bible offers solutions for us. Jacob sinned more than once, but he valued God's blessing, knowing it was more important than anything else. Eli and Saul show us what happens when disobedience rules. Elijah was rebuked for thinking he was the only faithful man left; however, he never gave up his trust in God. Along with his rebuke, God fed and refreshed Elijah with sleep. We may suffer the consequences of wrong decisions, but if we keep our focus on God, even our distress can bring good (Rom. 8:28).

Stages of Stress

Dr. Hans Selye, who first wrote at length about stress, constructed a theory called general adaptation syndrome (GAS for short). Selye, an endocrinologist, the director of the Institute of Experimental Medicine and Surgery, University of Montreal, and President of the International Institute of Stress suggests that stress has three stages.

Alarm — The body signals that it is under stress. During this stage, the autonomic nervous system creates an increase of hormone secretions by the adrenal glands. The Bible gives several examples of this stage of stress. Second Chronicles 20:3 tells of Jehoshaphat's alarm when he learns of the vast foreign army threatening their land. First Kings 1:49 reports the alarm felt by the guests of would-be-king Adonijah as Solomon was declared king instead of him. Psalm 31:22 says that David experienced alarm when cut off in a beseiged city. Second Samuel 4:1 reports that Ish-bosheth lost his courage and all Israel was alarmed.

Yet ironically, when referring to the catastrophes that will take place at the end of the world, Jesus says we should not be alarmed (Matthew 24:6). Paul writes Timothy that we do not possess a spirit of fear but of love, power, and a sound mind (1 Timothy 1:7).

Adaptation or Resistance — God made your body able to adapt to different types of stressful environments. When your body is cold, you shiver to generate heat. When your body is hot, you sweat. If there is too much light, your pupils contract. If there is not enough light, they dilate. If the sound is too loud, your ears actually adapt and temporarily turn the noise down. Maureen G. Mulvaney (author of several books on stress) says that "We face a multitude of real life stressors in everyday life. We have to choose whether to adapt to these stresses or not to adapt to them."

In this stage either the body's defenses win the battle or the stress continues for a longer period of time. The longer the stressor is present, the more the body's mechanism deteriorates. If this time period is too great, or the stressor increases beyond the body's resistance, exhaustion sets in.

Exhaustion — If the stress is unmanaged or persists too long, the body breaks down. This is true especially when the types of resistance chosen do not adequately deal with the stress (Dan. 8:27; Luke 22:45). At this time we are most vulnerable to attack by Satan (Luke 4:12). He is a roaring lion seeking to destroy (1 Peter 5:8). Stress provides an atmosphere for him to work destruction.

The Effects of Stress

In the following acrostic definiton you can see all these elements of time discussed in the previous section and the initial effect which stress has.

Situations
Temporarily
Reducing
Effectiveness
Sapping
Strength

Why does stress sap a person's strength? Stress is very frustrating, fatiguing, and enervating. It affects the immune system. Research by Selye from 1950-1956 showed that stress affects the heart, blood vessels, muscles, kidneys, and bones; in fact, it affects the entire body, attacking the weakest area first.

Consider these statements by Dr. Simonton concerning the effect stress has on the body. "The body is designed so that moments of stress, followed by a physical reaction such as fighting or fleeing do little harm. However, when the physiological response to stress is not discharged — because of the social consequences of "fighting" or "fleeing" — then there is a negative cumulative effect on the body. This is chronic stress, stress that is held in the body and not released. And chronic stress, it is increasingly recognized, plays a significant role in many illnesses" (O. Carl Simonton, M.D., Stephanie Matthews-Simonton, James L. Creighton, *Getting Well Again* [New York: Bantam Books, 1980], p. 44).

The part of the body that controls the reaction to stress is the autonomic nervous system. This system is broken down into two other systems: the sympathetic and the parasympathetic nervous systems. It is the sympathetic that prepares the body to fight or flee during times of stress. This system turns on the emotional responses of the body. It is the parasympathetic that calms the body down, that conserves energy, and builds up the resources of the body. This system turns down the body's emotional responses.

Stress drains a person's mental, physical, emotional, and spiritual energy. When the stress is too great, it creates physical exhaustion. Exhaustion occurs when the sympathetic nervous system is overactive and the parasympathetic nervous system is inactive. This in turn reduces a person's effectiveness in every area of life.

The sympathetic nervous system, when activated, orchestrates a whole series of physical responses in the body. Some of them are listed below:

> The lenses in the eyes focus for distance vision.
> Heart rate and force of contraction increases. The blood supply to the heart increases.
> The blood supply to the skin increases to maintain body temperature.
> Blood supply increases to the skeletal muscles.
> The hypothalamus tells the pituitary gland to secrete hormones into the blood stream, which activates the adrenal glands.
> The adrenal gland releases cortisol, epinephrine, and norepinephrine into the blood, which affects the body in many

ways. Epinephrine increases the force and speed of the heartbeat. Norepinephrine helps to maintain blood pressure.
➤ The brain, through a series of complex actions, makes sure it receives adequate blood supply and that the blood sugar level is high enough to maintain extra energy.

Stress produces a metabolic reaction in the body, affecting respiration rate, heart rate, and blood pressure; related to this is the effect of stress on the arteries. A report in the December 1997 journal of the American Heart Association, *Circulation*, shows a link between stress and blocked arteries. The 20% who experienced the greatest stress (measured by blood pressure changes) when taking cognitive and motor skill tests had thicker carotid artery walls. The thickness of the carotid artery wall is linked to an increased risk of heart attack.

Causes of Stress

Many words in our language are used to describe stress: strain, tense, laborious, difficult, burdensome, weighty, harassing, irksome, painful, troublesome. But they do not tell us why we are so prone to stress. I would like to suggest several situations which set us up for stress.

A) **Not being sure that what you are doing is right.** This probably occurs when you are trying to put together that new piece of furniture with 200 parts, or when you are completing your tax form. More seriously, it can occur when you have to make decisions that affect other people's welfare.

B) **Not being sure of what to do next.** Confusion and chaos are created by uncertainty. When you do not know what steps need to be taken to complete a task, you feel frustrated and tense. The level of stress depends on the gravity of the situation.

C) **Not being sure what priorities to give to the decisions you need to make.** Many people make lists of things to do, but they lack the wisdom to know which one is most important.

Suggested Solutions

In this, as in everything, make sure that you "first seek the counsel of the LORD" (1 Kings 22:5). Jehoshaphat, king of Judah, did this when he was in danger of being attacked by the Ammonite and Moabite armies. Second Chronicles 20:4 tells us, "The people of Judah came together to seek help from the LORD; indeed they came from every town in Judah to seek him."

Recognize that one of Satan's goals is to create self-doubt in you. He tried it on Eve with "Did God say . . . ? (Genesis 3:11), and it worked. He tried it on Jesus with "If you are the Son of God . . . " (Matthew 4:3, 6), but it did not work.

There are four other "right" questions that Satan uses to create doubt and stress in people's lives.

1. Are you doing it the right way?
2. Are you doing it for the right reason?
3. Are you the right person?
4. Are you doing God's right plan and will in your life?

People under this type of stress usually carry on an endless mental debate to find the "right" answers to the "right" questions. This internal conflict is extremely fatiguing. Being aware of Satan's tactics and seeking God and his wisdom as Jehoshaphat did are excellent ways to get rid of self-doubt.

Other solutions to be tried are these from the United Hospital, St. Paul, MN as printed in the *Grand Forks Herald*:

1. Don't withdraw; find social support. Be with people you enjoy, not just those you feel you should be with.
2. Avoid unrealistic expectations and demands on yourself. Make rational plans. Set priorities.
3. Relax your body. Breathe deeply. Exercise. Go limp for thirty seconds. Physical tension causes elevated heart rate and blood pressure.
4. Express your feelings. Don't pretend to be jolly if you're not. Be honest.

5. Don't overdo. Take breaks. Get enough rest. Eat right. Spend time doing something you enjoy.
6. Avoid too much of a good thing. Take some quiet time for yourself each day.

Keep in mind the admonition I received in a fortune cookie the other day: "You will emerge victorious from the maze you have been traveling in." When stress makes us feel we are walking a pathless maze, it is valuable to realize this truth: **eventually we will be victorious** (Rom. 8:37-39).

POINTS TO PONDER

Think of people mentioned in Scripture who experienced stress/ distress. List them and talk about their reasons for stress. Or answer the following.

1. What did God tell Abram to do in Genesis 12:1-9? How old was Abram? Did his age contribute to his stress?

2. What did Jacob do to Esau his twin brother that created stress, as recorded in Genesis 32:7-8? What action did Jacob take as a result of this? (Genesis 27:41-45).

3. As you think about the life of Joseph, count the different incidents that stressed him (Genesis 37:12-36; 39ff).

4. Moses indicates the stress he felt as he led the people out of Egypt (Numbers 11:10-15).

5. We know King Saul felt stress, for he had David play for him. What was the cause? (1 Samuel 28:15).

6. What reasons caused stress for David from the time he was anointed until he became king? How about after he became king? (1 Sam. 15–1 Kgs. 2:12).

7. What did Elijah have to feel stressed about? (1 Kings 19:2).

8. Esther heard some bad news which caused her deep distress. What was it? (Esther 4:4; 7:4).

9. Why did Job feel distressed? (Job 1).

10. What caused Jesus to break down and weep in distress? (Matt. 26:37; Luke 22:44).

11. Even King Herod felt distressed. Why? (Mark 6:21-29).

12. Paul writes much about his distress: 1 Thess. 3:7; 2 Cor 2:4; Acts 17:16; 2 Cor 11:24-28; 2 Cor. 6:4-5. List the different items which caused him stress.

Chapter 2
STRESS —
IS IT THE EVENT OR PERCEPTION?

Often it is not the event itself, but our perception of the event that causes stress. We put pressure on ourselves to work hard because we want to outdo someone else or reach a particular goal. Dr. Dean Ornish emphasizes: "Hard work doesn't give people heart attacks. Hard work itself can be good for you. But sometimes people think, 'If only I can make a certain amount of money,' or 'If only I can get this promotion,' or 'If only I can get this acknowledgment' — whatever it happens to be — then I'll be okay. Those motivations [self-imposed pressures] are what cause stress, which in turn can lead to illness."

Multiple Sources of Stress

✔ **Painful past** events create stress. Psychology refers to this as post-traumatic stress disorder (PTSD). Different kinds of past events can create present stress. A hazing experience in college, severe mental, physical, or sexual abuse, threats of bodily harm, involvement in war or witnessing a traumatic incident are only some of the past events that cause present stress.

✔ **The environment** we live in produces stress. The following six are not exhaustive.

    1) *heat-cold (temperature)*

        at 70–80 degrees Farenheit the number of hours before
        • performance declines is approximately five hours.

        at 80–90 degrees Farenheit the number of hours before
        performance declines is approximately two hours.

        at 90–100 degrees Farenheit the number of hours before
        performance declines is approximately one hour.
        (Adapted from J.F. Wing, "Upper Tolerance Limits for
        Unimpaired Mental Performance," *Aerospace Medicine*,
        36 [1965], pp. 960-964.)

    2) *noise pressure (intensity, as well as kind, e.g., phone)*

Research has shown that when the level and duration of the noise is reduced, this produces a healthier work place and affects performance positively. Music has been linked to improved performance. (J.G. Fox, "Background music and industrial productivity: A review," *Applied Ergonomics*, 2 [1971], pp. 70-73).

> High levels of noise have been shown to lead to an increase in blood pressure and other signs of stress. In noisy surroundings, such as in the midtown area during times of heavy traffic, people appear less aware of the distress of others and are less inclined to offer help. High noise levels also seem to impair learning, a particular problem for inner-city children.
> (Spencer A. Rathus and Jeffrey S. Nevid, *Adjustment and Growth* [New York: Holt, Rinehart and Winston, 1983], p. 405.)

    3) *radiation, illumination, lighting levels*

Lighting: Bright lights when accompanied by glare, give people more headaches and eyestrain, affecting performance at work negatively. (E.J. McCormick, *Human Factors Engineering*, 2nd ed. [New York: McGraw-Hill, 1964]).

    4) *weather conditions*

I live in what is considered "tornado alley." In central Indiana, the spring and summer are considered tornado season.

This time of year can be very stressful emotionally. I know many people who have a hard time sleeping during thunderstorms. They are anxious when the storm warnings are set off by the National Weather Service.

I know many people who are "stressed out" during winter. They hate getting out because it is gray outside. At times this condition might be called "Seasonal Affective Disorder." Many times in the winter in central Indiana we will go for days, possibly weeks without seeing the sun. The cloud cover prevents the sun from shining through. This is highly stressful and depressive.

5) *colors in the work place*

Blues and greens have been found to have a soothing effect.

Red tends to excite.

Yellows and oranges tend to increase alertness and attention span.

Gray tends to depress.

6) *crowds*

Jesus was often around large crowds. This had to create stress for him. Matthew wrote about Jesus, "When he saw the crowds, he had compassion on them, because they were harassed and helpless, like sheep without a shepherd" (Matthew 9:36). Jesus was almost crushed by a crowd (Luke 8:42). Luke also records, "Yet the news about him spread all the more, so that crowds of people came to hear him and to be healed of their sicknesses. But Jesus often withdrew to lonely places and prayed" (Luke 5:15-16).

✔ **Our physical bodies are prone to**:

chronic pain

breakdowns because of growing old

illness and disease

All diseases can be very stressful to the body. They disrupt the cycle of the body, which leads to more stress. Not only is the disease itself stressful, it is also stressful because of the amount of money it costs to treat the disease. Illness then can become a double-edged stress sword.

✔ **Thoughts**: The way people think and what they think creates stress. Stress is also created because we think too much! Many people have this problem. Overthinking is the cause of restless, sleepless nights and emotionally draining days. Frequently a great debate goes on within our heads about decisions we need to make. This debate only creates chaos and confusion which lead to stress.

Most stress is not caused by the situation, but from perceptions and thoughts about the situation. Thoughts cause your body to respond to stress in stressful ways. This will be discussed at length in chapter 5.

As a person thinks about his particular situation, he may dwell on his own failure until he feels utterly hopeless. This negative emotion is caused by his perception; the situation may not be hopeless at all. Unrealistic expectations of self or others cause frustration, anger, and even bitterness. One who is a perfectionist may refuse to admit failure and blame others so that hostility results. All of these negative emotions result in stress, and they are brought about by the thought process of the individual.

✔ **Loneliness/singleness** One of the most stressful things about being lonely is frequently there is no one with whom to talk or share. We need someone to whom we can express our hopes, dreams, expectations and disappointments. I hear guys especially say, "I like being single and alone." I don't believe this is aways true, in spite of the number of times I hear it.

We live in a couple's world. To many people, the single state signals that something is wrong. The single person may think, "If only I were smarter, more beautiful, had a different personality, I wouldn't be single." This thought pattern can be deadly because it creates massive amounts of anger, fear, and stress on top of the stress of having to handle life without a companion. Satan loves, encourages, and teaches this thought pattern, for he likes nothing better than accusing you to youself.

Cardiologist and author Stephen T. Sinatra says that heartache contributes to heart disease and heart attacks, both signs and symptoms of stress, in his book *Heartbreak and Heart Disease: A Mind/Body Prescription for Healing the Heart.*

Roy Baumeister, Ph.D., and Elsie B. Smith, professor at Case Western Reserve University in Ohio, have done research on college students and relationship breakups. They found that students who had recently experienced a breakup had more sore throats and colds, manifested poorer immune responses, drank more, and about 50% of them had a measurably lower self-esteem (Condensed from Roberta Pollack Seid, Ph.D., "Heart-break Hotel," Joe Weider's *Shape* magazine [September 1997], p. 56.)

An ABC news broadcast said this about loneliness, "A nine-year study by reasearchers at the University of California shows that loneliness has a greater impact on the death rate than smoking, drinking, eating, or exercise. The study found that people without spouses or friends had a death rate twice as high as those with social ties" (J. Oswald Sanders, *Facing Loneliness,* [Grand Rapids: Discovery House Publishers, 1990], p. 49).

Tim Timmons, author of *Loneliness Is Not a Disease,* wrote, "More people are feeling lonely. Their lives consist of proximity without presence, relationship without contact, and familiarity without feelings." Timmons also wrote, "Once a philo-sophical problem contemplated by poets and prophets, loneli-ness is now a universal condition for millions of Americans. Not only for the elderly and divorced, but also for the men and women filled with the ache of loneliness within their marriages. It is fast becoming an American tradition."

Albert Einstein said, "It is strange to be known so univer-sally, and yet to be so lonely." Lily Tomlin said, "We're all in this together — by ourselves." David wrote on the issue of loneliness, "Look upon my affliction and my distress" (Psalm 25:18). The words found in this passage are "afflicted," "troubles multi-plied," "anguish," and "affliction." These words greatly describe loneliness.

Being single for most people is an undesired experience. Aristotle said, "Friendship is a thing most necessary to life — since without friends, no one would choose to live, though pos-sessed of all other advantages" (Sanders, *Facing Loneliness*, p. 149).

Solomon wrote about loneliness and singleness, "Two are better than one, because they have a good return for their work: If one falls down, his friend can help him up. But pity the man who falls and has no one to help him up! Also, if two lie down together, they will keep warm. But how can one keep warm alone? Though one may be overpowered, two can defend them-selves. A cord of three strands is not quickly broken" (Eccl. 4:9). These verses describe how stressful loneliness can be.

God speaks the first negative in Scripture regarding loneli-ness, "It is not good for the man to be alone. I will make a helper suitable for him" (Gen. 2:18). Although Adam was in fel-lowship with God, God knew that Adam was still alone. God saw loneliness as a condition that needed to be remedied. A person alone has four negative, stressful reactions (Eccl. 4:10-12).

1) He has no one to help him with tasks or projects.
2) This person does not have a good return for his work.
3) He can't keep warm by himself.
4) He can be easily overpowered.

Many people in the Bible experienced loneliness:
Adam — Genesis 2:18
Jacob — Genesis 32:23-30
Joseph — Genesis 43:30-31
Jeremiah — Jeremiah 15:17
Nehemiah — Nehemiah 1:12-16
Daniel — Daniel 10:8
Paul — 2 Timothy 4:16
David — Psalm 25:16-18

Another possible source of stress for a single person is the possibility of having no children. For that matter, being married and not being able to have children can create a tremendous amount of stress. Battling through infertility problems can be a time of great stress. A woman wrote, "There are lonely times. I face never being called 'Mom' or 'Grandma.' I have a deep ache when I see my husband's pain — no child runs to him calling, 'Daddy!'" (Joy E. DeKok, "Infertility — The Death of a Dream," *Decision* [November 1997], pp. 14-15).

Many single people also want children. This lack of children is very stressful and frequently makes people feel worthless. Esteem for women is frequently associated with the ability to bear children. The converse, abortion on demand, creates anger and stress for people who want to have kids but can't. Anger may also stem from the prolonged agony of trying to adopt children and having a small adoptive pool available, as well as the cost associated with it.

Two people in Scripture come to mind as I write about this type of stress and anger: Rachel and Hannah. Rachel was so distressed she said to Jacob, "Give me children, or I'll die" (Gen. 30:1). Hannah told Eli the priest, "I am a woman who is deeply troubled. I have not been drinking wine or beer; I was pouring out my soul to the LORD. Do not take your servant for a wicked woman; I have been praying here out of my great anguish and grief" (1 Sam. 1:15-16). This deep trouble was the result of her not being able to have a son.

Hannah made a vow to God about this issue, "O LORD Almighty, if you will only look upon your servant's misery and remember me, and not forget your servant but give her a son, then I will give him to the LORD for all the days of his life, and no razor will ever be used on his head" (1 Sam. 1:11). She was serious about her vow because this is exactly what she did when Samuel was born.

Loneliness and loss can be life threatening. In a study conducted in 1969, of 4500 British widowers, it was found that they had a 40% higher death rate within six months of their wives' deaths compared to other men of the same age. (Braun and Linder, *Psychology Today*, p. 343). What God said about this issue is true, "It is not good for the man to be alone. I will make a helper suitable for him" (Gen. 2:18). God knew before 1969 that lonely and grieving people would have a harder life.

✔ **The physical and chemical environment** in which we live is stressful to the body. Allergies, bacteria and viruses are found everywhere. Many people are prone to them. These things can easily be found in the environment in which we live. The recent strep outbreak in Texas and Illinois which killed people caused fear and stress for the people in those areas.

All toxic substances, poisons, drugs, medications, chemical additives found in food can produce stress. Excesses in the use of alcohol, nicotine, and caffeine can also produce stress. These substances, when abused, cause stress for the body, as well as emotional stress.

✔ **The Work Atmosphere** is frequently a place where stress exists. Stress at work is often created by several employment situations:

1. Being responsible for tasks being completed.
2. Being accountable to someone for the task to be completed.
3. Being in a situation where you have no authority over others who are working on the task to be completed.
4. Receiving no praise or compliments when the task is completed.
5. Not having clear expectations of performance from coworkers, supervisors, and management.
6. Lack of control of decisions about workload and scheduling of work hours.
7. Limited job advancement, small pay raises, and low wages.
8. Multiple bosses who place different expectations and demands on workers.
9. Value conflicts with coworkers and bosses.
10. Rapid changes in technology, workload and responsibilities.

11. Changes in management personnel and style of management.
12. Problems with child care during work hours.
13. Worry about children when at work and concern about sick children.
14. Backbiting by bosses and coworkers. This is often referred to as "office politics."

The type of job makes a difference in stress level as well. High pressure jobs tend to create more stress than low pressure ones. Professional athletes understand stress. When a free throw wins the game, or a putt gives the golfer a huge pay check, stress is present. The pressure under these circumstances is incredible. This is why you hear announcers say, "He choked under the pressure." Frequently many professional sports have victory or defeat hanging on the last 30 seconds of the game. This is a pressure packed time. This could be why many professional athletes struggle with alcohol and drug abuse.

I identify six jobs that are highly stressful in today's world. Three are in the medical field; doctors, nurses and medical personnel. These people work in an environment where life and death hang in the balance and are part of their job descriptions. Three other jobs that carry a lot of stress are an air traffic controller, law enforcement officer and firefighter. The stress is created by the fact that people's lives rest in their hands. Police and firefighters also have to deal with their own possible deaths as well. Welcome to stress at its highest degree!

Any work environment can be stressful, though, due to the fact that "downsizing" and "layoffs" are common words in the workplace today. Recently Muncie, Indiana, has had a couple of factories close and one company move its headquarters to Colorado. One thousand six hundred jobs were lost. This has created a lot of stress in Muncie. I am sure that many people are worried about the possibility of losing their jobs next.

Not only do people have to worry about losing their jobs, but several have to make decisions about whether they should move with the company or stay in town and look for new employment. Moving means having to sell a house in what may be a depressed housing market because of the job losses, having to find a new house and putting the kids in a new school system in a totally new state, and having to leave friends and family. Staying means possibly not being able to find a new job or taking a job with less pay. People in this type of circumstance can easily feel overwhelmed by the decisions they have to make. Frequently people can think they are in a no-win situation, that any decision they make is wrong. Welcome to stress.

In the 1960s Dr. Sidney Cobb studied 200 laid-off auto workers from Detroit for two years. He found that during the time of the layoffs several suffered depression, high blood pressure, ulcers, arthritis, and their suicide rate was thirty times higher than the average (Braun and Linder, *Psychology Today*, p. 343).

Many people work in jobs that have high performance pressure and are very insecure. Many people work where criticism is all they hear from their supervisors. Any work environment where there is a lack of compliments is highly stressful.

Several other factors make the work environment stressful: time pressure, workers being overtaxed with demands, job insecurity and poor personal relationships with bosses and coworkers. Research shows that "the greater the job satisfaction, the lower is the likelihood of coronary disease" (Benjamin Kleinmuntz, *Essentials of Abnormal Psychology* [New York: Harper and Row, 1974], p. 214).

People can also work in situations where they are being underutilized. The skills that they have are not being used to the greatest potential. This tends to create boredom, which is a form of stress. People can also work in environments where they are being overutilized. They are being stretched to their limits daily. This environment will create burnout, which is also stressful to the human body.

Here are the top 10 headache makers in the nation, according to Excedrin's survey of 1205 adults:
1. Not getting enough sleep.
2. Having too much to do in too little time.
3. Kids getting on the nerves.
4. Not eating right.
5. Facing the cost of living.
6. Paying the bills.
7. Dealing with the overwhelming workload.
8. Coping with pressure to start saving more.
9. Spending too much; needing to cut back.
10. Arguing with the spouse.
(Georgea Kovanis, Knight-Ridder Newspapers)

P⊕INTS T⊕ P⊕NDER

1. What environmental factors affect you the most in reference to stress? What can you do about them?

2. Do you carry on internal debates? What about? How can you deal with them?

3. What thought patterns do you have that cause stress? Can you change your thoughts? Does Phil. 4:8 offer a solution?

4. Why does loneliness set us up for stress? Can the friendship of fellow believers help alleviate this stress? What else can a person do?

5. Are there stress factors at the place you work? Are they manageable or over the limits? What solution might you find for them?

6. Rate the top 10 headache makers in the nation on a scale of one to ten as they affect your life.

Chapter 3
HOW VULNERABLE ARE YOU TO STRESS?

As I wrote in the previous chapter, our bodies are prone to illness and disease. This weakness came into the world after sin. Before sin, there was no illness in the garden. But, after sin, man's body has been prone to illnesses that destroy it. But God is aware of our weakness. David writes, "For he remembers that we are dust" (Ps. 103:14).

Prevalent Stressors

- Inadequate diet and irregularity of eating habits
- Insufficient sleep
- Inadequate exercise
- Inability to relax
- Ignorance of the components of healthy living
- Insufficient recreation
- Lack of genuine intimacy
- Lack of planning and order of work life and personal life
- Harsh demands on self
- Unrealistic expectations from others

- Lack of self-awareness
- Neglect of self-care
- Depending on things and others for self worth
- Holding conflicting beliefs about the same subject
- Breaking of a personal value

Change is one of the most stressful parts of life. Below is a diagram of change that shows there are eight types of change. All change is stressful, but some changes are more stressful and difficult than others. Let's look at the types of change.

Wanted	**Unwanted**
Sudden Unexpected	Sudden Unexpected
Expected	Expected
Gradual	Gradual

Which side (wanted or unwanted) is the most stressful? Most of the people would say it is the "unwanted." One of the things about life that fascinates me is that most change is unwanted. People's health changes unwantedly. Job losses and downsizing are usually unwanted. Having to put a parent in a nursing home is unwanted and highly stressful. Talk about a time when Satan will attack with doubt! I can only imagine what kind of stress this must cause for the children of these parents who have to wrestle with this decision. Luke 4:13 gives us insight into Satan's timing of attacks, "When the devil had finished all this tempting, he left him until an opportune time."

Which level (sudden unexpected, expected or gradual) is the most stressful? This depends on your personality. I believe that all three of these create stress. But what is stressful to one person may not be stressful to another. Some good illustrations of this would be going to the dentist or flying. I know many people who find going to the dentist actually enjoyable. I know several people who avoid dentists and flying at all costs!

How a person handles stress, and whether a person gets stressed in certain situations may depend a lot on the personality. Recent research has come up with a personality profile for a person who is more likely to suffer a second heart attack. This personality is called "type D." It stands for "distressed personality." In the past it was believed that type A personalities had a greater chance of heart problems. Dr. Friedman and Dr. Rosenman wrote a book titled *Type A Behavior and Your Heart* which discussed how different personalities handle emotional and mental situations. Type A people were constantly on the move; type B were the laid-back, relaxed individuals. Type D personality is a fairly new diagnosis. Type D people tend to be inhibited socially, negative in thought process, and insecure.

Anything different, even positive, can create stress! Why is this? Any time a person goes into a different situation, Satan is an opportunist (Luke 4:13). Satan will take times like these to create self-doubt. He knows that as people change careers, they may doubt that they did the right thing. He knows they may think that maybe they "bit off more than they can chew." This thought creates a lot of stress.

Who in the Bible Went through Change?

Adam and Eve: The obvious change of residence, being kicked out of the garden, had to create stress for Adam and Eve, along with the change of having to struggle to make a living and to trust each other again. Solomon wrote in Psalm 127:2 about this type of stress, "In vain you rise early and stay up late, toiling for food to eat . . . ." There was also an increase in the pain of childbirth for Eve that created stress (Gen. 3:16).

Jacob: Multiple changes of residence and living circumstances; change of name from "Grasper" to "Contender with God"

Abraham: Change of living situation

David: Shepherd to King

33

King Saul: King to ex-king
Paul: Change of name; change of religion — Jew to Christian
Peter: Change of name and occupation
Disciples: Change of occupation

Can you think of others who went through changes?

It is important that you are aware of events (changes) that can create stress. Drs. Thomas H. Holmes and R.H. Rahe, at the University of Washington School of Medicine, came up with the social readjustment scale (Source: Thomas H. Holmes and Richard H. Rahe, "The Social Readjustment Rating Scale," *Journal of Psychosomatic Research* [1967], pp. 213-218).

Social Readjustment Rating Scale

Events	Points
1. Death of spouse	100
2. Divorce	73
3. Marital separation	65
4. Jail term	63
5. Death of a close family member	63
6. Personal illness or injury	53
7. Marriage	50
8. Fired from work	47
9. Marriage reconciliation	45
10. Retirement	45
11. Change in a family member's health	44
12 Pregnancy	40
13. Sex difficulties	39
14. Gain of a new family member	39
15 Business readjustment	39
16. Change in financial status	38
17. Death of close friend	37
18 Change to a different line of work	36
19. Change in number of arguments with spouse	35
20. Mortgage or loan *over* $10,000.00	31
21. Foreclosure of mortgage or loan	30
22 Change in responsibilities at work	29
23. Son or daughter leaving home	29

Drs. T.H. Holmes and R.H. Rahe state that future illnesses are more likely to occur after people have experienced high levels of stress. They found that forty-nine percent of people who had 300 or more points within a twelve-month period reported illness during the period of the study. Only nine percent reported illness during the study period if they scored below 200. The results of this test also revealed that eighty percent of those who scored 300 points or more would experience depression and illness within the next two years.

2,300 women from 20 states were asked how they were affected by the events in the original study. The "new" top ten list (Sorry, David Letterman) are:

New Rank	Stressor	Old Rank
1	Death of a spouse	1
2	Divorce	2
3	Marriage	7

4	Death of close family member	5
5	Fired from job	8
6	Marital separation	3
7	Pregnancy	12
8	Jail term	4
9	Death of a close friend	17
10	Retirement	10

Source: Gary J. Oliver, Ph.D., and H. Norman Wright, *Good Women Get Angry* (Ann Arbor, MI: Servant Publications, 1995), p. 133.

Rating for New Stressors

Stressor	Points
Disabled child	97
Single parenting	96
Remarriage	89
Depression	89
Abortion	89
Child's illness	87
Infertility	87
Spouse's illness	85
Crime victimization	84
Husband's retirement	82
Parenting parents	81
Raising teens	80
Chemical dependency	80
Parent's illness	78
Singleness	77

Source: Oliver and Wright, *Good Women Get Angry*, p. 134.

Here is a recent survey that I found in our local paper.

"Stressed out? Here's why (Knight Ridder Newspapers) *The StarPress*, Muncie, IN August 29, 1999, page 4E

A survey in June of 400 people nationwide identified these as the 10 most stressful issues in the past 12 months:
1. Learning to use the Internet
2. Gun violence and kids

3. Waiting to see *Star Wars: Episode I — The Phantom Menace*
4. China stealing U.S. military secrets
5. The JonBenet Ramsey murder case
6. Michael Jordan retiring
7. Airing NBC's final episode of *Seinfeld*
8. Hillary Clinton's potential U.S. Senate candidacy
9. Y2K
10. Plane crashes in the news

Do any of these surprise you? Does the order surprise you? What may be stressful to one person, may be laughable to another. I rejoiced when Michael Jordan retired since I am a Pacers fan!

There are five biblical "R"s of stress management. I would encourage you to pray for these things daily, especially during times of change and stress.

What does God want to do for us? He wants to:

Refresh (Ps. 68:9; 2 Pet. 1:12-13)

Restore (Ps. 23:3; 51:12; 53:6; 80:3,7,19; 85:4)

Revive (Ps. 19:7; 85:6)

Renew (Ps. 51:10; Isa. 40:31) Psalm 103:5 tells us the Lord is the one, "who satisfies your desires with good things so that your youth is renewed like the eagle's." I see eagles as being strong creatures that are capable of great heights and wonderful flights. What a great visual picture of what getting rid of stress feels like.

Rebuild (Ps. 69:35)

The spirit, soul and body are refreshed, restored, revived, renewed, and rebuilt in five ways.

Nutrition — Elijah needed food to deal with his stress. The angel that ministered to him knew this.

Then he lay down under the tree and fell asleep. All at once an angel touched him and said, "Get up and eat." He looked around, and there by his head was a cake of bread baked over hot coals, and a jar of water. He ate and drank and then lay down again. The angel of the LORD came back a second time and touched him and said, "Get up and eat, for the journey is too much for you." So he got up and ate and drank. Strengthened by that food, he traveled forty days and forty nights until he reached Horeb, the mountain of God (1 Kgs. 19:5-8).

Sleep —Sleep is becoming more important all the time. March 30–April 5th, 1998 was the first annual National Sleep Awareness Week. It was sponsored by the National Sleep Foundation. Their website address is *www.sleepfoundation.org.* This week was designed to promote good sleeping habits by doing the largest public poll ever on sleep and related issues. The goal of this week was to encourage Americans to get eight hours of sleep a night.

The Bible discusses the importance of sleep. David wrote, "I will lie down and sleep in peace, for you alone, O LORD, make me dwell in safety" (Ps. 4:8). He also wrote, "I lie down and sleep; I wake again, because the LORD sustains me" (Ps. 3:5). Solomon wrote "It is vain for you to rise up early, To retire late, To eat the bread of painful labors; For He gives to His beloved even in his sleep (Ps. 127:2, NASB). The New International Version says it, "In vain you rise early and stay up late, toiling for food to eat — for he grants sleep to those he loves."

Sleep appears then to be a major component in the handling of stress on the physical body. Recent studies have shown that animals when deprived of sleep for 17 days die. Thom Geier in *US News and World Report*, (August 18/25, 1997, p. 48) wrote an excellent article on the mysteries of sleep. He says that some research on sleep suggests that sleep "might be a means of boosting the immune system to ward off disease."

Good, sufficient sleep is as important to the vitality of life and good health as exercise and diet. Sleep loss affects the body mentally, socially, spiritually, and physically. The proper amount of sleep can aid in stress reduction. Some things you can do to sleep better are:

➤ Get eight hours of sleep a night.

It is perfectly all right to take naps during your day. Winston Churchill took a nap during the afternoon while

HOW VULNERABLE ARE YOU?

he was wartime Prime Minister of England. Many US Presidents have also napped. Calvin Coolidge, John Kennedy, and Lyndon Johnson all napped. Napoleon even napped on the battlefield.

➤ Avoid decongestants, caffeine, nicotine and alcohol.
➤ Don't exercise before you go to bed.
➤ Don't eat a big meal right before bed time.
➤ Don't think about your concerns and worries just before bedtime.
➤ Try to go to bed and get up at the same times each day.

Exercise — This is one of the best ways to relieve stress. Exercise increases the production of endorphins in the body. Endorphins are the body's natural painkillers. These polypeptides are produced in the brain. They are like opiates that produce analgesia (Greek "*an*" not; "*algos*" pain). "According to the American College of Sports Medicine, to improve your aerobic fitness, you need to exercise for 20-60 consecutive minutes three to five days a week at 60-90 percent of your maximum heart rate." (Joe Weider's *Shape* magazine, September 1997, page 101.)

Laughter — Solomon wrote that laughter is the best medicine (Prov.17:22). Laughter is a free, universal medicine that aids the body in a number of ways. This will be discussed in detail later in this study.

Fellowship — This is probably one of the most overlooked areas of refreshment to the stressed spirit of man. The Bible teaches much about fellowship. The writer of Hebrews wrote, "Let us not give up meeting together, as some are in the habit of doing, but let us encourage one another — and all the more as you see the Day approaching" (Heb. 10:25). Paul wrote, "Share with God's people who are in need. Practice hospitality" (Rom. 12:13). He also wrote, "Rejoice with those who rejoice; mourn with those who mourn" (Rom. 12:15). What a great explanation of how to fellowship with other Christians!

The Greek New Testament word for fellowship is "*koinonia*," meaning sharing, partnership, and contribution. The word is not frequently used in the New Testament. In Acts 2:42-47 Luke wrote,

> They devoted themselves to the apostles' teaching and to the fellowship, to the breaking of bread and to prayer. Everyone was filled with awe, and many wonders and miraculous signs were done by the apostles. All the believers were together and had everything in common. Selling their possessions and goods, they gave to anyone as he had need. Every day they continued to meet together in the temple courts. They broke bread in their homes and ate together with gladness and sincere hearts, praising God and enjoying the favor of all the people. And the Lord added to their number daily those who were being saved.

Paul wrote, "For Macedonia and Achaia were pleased to make a contribution for the poor among the saints in Jerusalem" (Rom. 15:26). In 1 Corinthians 1:9 Paul wrote, "God, who has called you into fellowship with his Son Jesus Christ our Lord, is faithful."

Other passages where this word is found are 1 Corinthians 10:16; 2 Corinthians 6:14; 8:4; 9:13; 13:14; Galatians 2:9; Ephesians 3:9; Philippians 1:5; 2:1; 3:10; Philemon 6; Hebrews 13:16; 1 John 1:3,6-7.

There are many other passages that tell us how we should treat one another in fellowship. Jesus said it best in Matthew 7:12, "Do to others as you would have them do to you." Paul taught that we should:

Romans 12:10
1. "be devoted to one another in brotherly love"
2. honor one another (Phil. 2:3-4)

Romans 12:16
1. live in harmony with one another

Romans 15:7
1. accept one another

Romans 15:14
1. instruct one another

Galatians 5:13
1. serve one another

Ephesians 4:2
    1. be patient with one another, bear with one another
Ephesians 4:32
    1. be kind to one another
    2. be compassionate to one another
Colossians 3:13
    1. bear with one another
    2. forgive one another
Colossians 3:16
    1. admonish one another
1 Thessalonians 5:11
    1. encourage one another

Several other passages in the Bible also deal with this idea.

Hebrews 10:24
    1. spur one another on toward love and good deeds
Hebrews 3:13; 10:25
    1. encourage one another
James 4:11
    1. do not slander one another
1 Peter 1:22
    1. love one another deeply
1 Peter 3:8 (Col. 3:12)
    1. live in harmony with one another
    2. be sympathetic with one another
    3. be compassionate with one another
1 Peter 5:5
    1. be humble with one another
1 John 1:7
    1. have fellowship with one another
1 John 3:11,23; 4:7,11; 2 John 5
    1. love one another

If we lived out these commands in fellowship with Christians, the potential for the refreshment of the spirit, soul and body would be phenomenal. Stress would definitely be reduced.

The Bible teaches that fellowship refreshes us. In Proverbs 11:25 Solomon wrote, "A generous man will prosper; he who refreshes others will himself be refreshed." Paul wrote, "By all this we are encouraged. In addition to our own encouragement, we were especially delighted to see how happy Titus was, because his spirit has been refreshed by all of you" (2 Cor. 7:13). Paul wrote earlier to the same Church, "I was glad when Stephanas, Fortunatus and Achaicus arrived, because they have supplied what was lacking from you. For they refreshed my spirit and yours also. Such men deserve recognition" (1 Cor. 16:17-18). Paul wrote to the Church at Rome, ". . . so that by God's will I may come to you with joy and together with you be refreshed" (Rom. 15:32). Paul wrote to Timothy, "May the Lord show mercy to the household of Onesiphorus, because he often refreshed me and was not ashamed of my chains" (2 Tim. 1:16).

How many of the above five refreshers surprised you as ways of healing the spirit, soul, and body of man? I suspect that it was coming with joy and showing mercy that surprised you the most. It is frequently these last two that get overlooked, and that is why there is a breakdown. We tend to use only 60% of what refreshes us. This could mean that only 60% gets refreshed. This will be discussed more in chapters 6 and 7 of this study.

POINTS TO PONDER

1. How vulnerable are you to stress?

2. How do you think Jesus would have done in the areas discussed in this chapter?

3. Why is it that under stress we neglect the things that help us deal with stress?

4. How does talking openly about your stresses and frustration help you deal with stress?

Chapter 4
Symptoms of Stress

Medical science for years has used physical signs and symptoms to diagnose illness and disease. When God created the body, He gave it a great warning system to present and future problems. When the body gets hot, this could be a signal that some virus is attacking the system. The body also gives many clues that it is under stress. Some signs, symptoms, and causes of stress are:

➤ An unexplained change in your effectiveness and performance.

➤ A pattern of absence from the stress-causing event.

➤ Cooled relationships

➤ Thwarted ambition — apathy (lack of interest or emotion); loss of creativity, imagination and risk taking.

➤ The fear that as you grow older, your capabilities are waning.

➤ Personality clashes, changes in number of fights, becoming easily defensive.

➤ Doing something that compromises or violates your conscience. Or being around things that violate your conscience (Rom. 14:15). Another stressor is having what you consider to be good spoken of as if it were evil (Rom. 14:16). David wrote, "Streams of tears flow from my eyes, for your law is not obeyed" (Ps. 119:136) He was grieving because of all the evil he saw in his society. We should grieve over all the things in our society that disobey God's laws. This grieving is very stressful, but healthy for a Christian.

Consider the example I gave before: You are thinking about placing a parent in the nursing home when it is against that parent's wishes. You may feel that you have let him down if you do it, but you feel it is in your parent's best interest — this is highly stressful. Being in a situation where you have to make a decision, feeling that whatever you decide is wrong and that it will have a negative outcome, is very stressful.

People in Compromising Situations

Lot: Genesis 13:12-13
                19:1-29
Samson: Judges 16:1-21
Solomon: 1 Kings 11:1-14
Asa: 2 Chronicles 16:1-9
Jehoshaphat: 2 Chronicles 18:1-3
                          19:1-2
                          20:35-37

Signs of Stress Should Not Be Ignored

My car has lights all over the dashboard. I can tell when my car is overheating, needs oil, or the battery is not charging properly. These lights, referred to as "warning lights" or "idiot lights," can be used to monitor the wear and tear on the vehicle. These lights can also be ignored and overlooked. This can have traumatic consequences to both the driver and auto. Our body also gives us "warning lights" about the wear and tear that stress has caused. These signs, like the dashboard lights, can be overlooked. The consequences of overlooking these signs can be devastating.

Dr. Simonton writes,

To start with, chronic stress frequently produces hormonal imbalances. Since hormones play a critical role in the regulating of the body functions, these imbalances can lead to high blood pressure and eventually damage to the kidneys. The damage to the kidneys can, in turn, lead to severe hypertension, (high blood pressure), which will reinforce the chemical imbalance.

In addition, the hormonal changes resulting from stress can allow tears to develop in the walls of arteries. The body repairs these tears by a buildup of cholesterol plaques, a type of scar tissue. But too many plaques cause hardening of the arteries, arteriosclerosis. This, in turn, forces the heart to pump harder to circulate the blood, further increasing the blood pressure. When arteriosclerosis becomes far advanced, it diminishes the amount of blood and oxygen reaching the heart to the point that coronary failure may occur. The cholesterol plaques may also block the heart's major coronary arteries, causing part of the heart muscle to die, resulting in eventual heart failure. Normally, the body will make an effort to adjust to these problems, but under chronic stress the mechanisms responsible for reducing and adjusting hormonal imbalance are overriden. The imbalance just continues in an increasingly negative and life-threatening cycle.

(From Simonton, Matthews-Simonton, and Creighton, *Getting Well Again*, pp. 44-45.)

Physical Signs of Stress

muscle tension	hives and rashes
muscle spasms	rapid heart rate, increase of heart rate, palpitations
problems sleeping, not getting rested	change in appetite, change in weight
lump in throat, difficulty swallowing	shallow breathing, breathlessness
diarrhea, constipation	dizziness, fainting

muscle weakness

high blood pressure

lower back pain

insomnia

flare-ups in preexisting conditions

  arthritis

  asthma

  peptic ulcers

  herpes

  lupus

  TMJ

  multiple sclerosis

  diabetes

  cold sores

hypertension

allergies

lower resistance to colds

lower energy

grinding teeth, clenching teeth

stomach problems

indigestion

headaches, migraines

choked feelings

backache, neck ache

increase in nervous mannerisms

excessive perspiration, sweaty palms and feet

sexual impotence

Emotional Signs of Stress

persistent sadness

depression

gloominess; pessimism

irritability

paranoia, fears

outbursts of anger

emotional withdrawal

strong anxiety

suicidal thoughts

loss of motivation

problem with being still or quiet

nervousness

aggression

helplessness

hopelessness

impaired concentration

mental confusion

feeling short of time

impatience

feeling that things are out of control

frustration

Thought Patterns and Stress

loss of memory

thinking everything's a catastrophe

racing thoughts

being critical of self and others

repetitive thoughts

feeling that people don't like you, paranoia

stubbornness

How People Act under Stress

always in a hurry	speak and eat quickly
can't sit for long	

How People React under Stress

hate losing	can't forget the situation
eat to calm down	drink to calm down
smoke to calm down	

As we close this chapter, consider this story that tells how people deal with stress differently.

"Differences among women in how they handle stress" *The Evening Press*, Muncie, IN (December 31, 1994) p. 14.

NEW YORK (AP) — Wherever in the world they live, women share similar concerns about money, family, health and other topics — but there are regional differences.

A new survey of women editors from 15 countries indicated that 88 percent reported high stress levels in their countries.

To relieve stress, North American women generally exercise, Latin Americans shop and Europeans eat or watch television.

P⊕INTS T⊕ P⊕NDER

1. What caused David to be bowed down in distress in Psalm 57:6? In Psalm 38:6?

2. Why did he cry out in distress in Psalm 55:17?

3. What kind of person suffers terror and anxiety as described in Job 15:24?

4. What caused Hezekiah to call his situation "a day of distress . . ." (Isa. 37:3)?

5. What brings the distress upon David in Psalm 25:16-19?

6. How does the writer of Psalm 119:143 deal with his distress?

7. List the troubles suffered by the writer of Psalm 88:1-18. Does it describe your state of mind?

8. How do you react under stress?
   Some common reactions:
   eating to calm down
   smoking to calm down
   drinking to calm down
   going over the troubling situation

9. Does Psalm 89:1-2 offer a way out of stress?

Chapter 5
THE FOUR EMOTIONAL STRONGHOLDS

Emotions are frequently a sign of stress, but they can also cause stress. This chapter will address four of the more common stress-creating emotions. Let's begin with some discussion on the ways in which a person develops.

Luke, who was a physician, states in Luke 2:52 that Jesus grew in four areas:

wisdom	(mental)
stature	(physical)
favor with God	(spiritual)
favor with man	(social)

These four aspects of development were perfectly balanced in Jesus and offer us an example of the wholeness God wants us to achieve.

Another Scripture, 1 Thessalonians 5:23, divides man into spirit, soul, and body. These three parts of man are under constant attack and oppression by the devil (Prov. 15:15; Dan. 7:25; Isa. 58:6) and are prone to stress and affliction. Notice the order of these three parts. Medical science tends to put them in reverse order: body, soul, and spirit.

Consider the following quote from William Saroyan, in the *Human Comedy*, "Doctors don't understand everything really.

They understand matter, not spirit. And you and I live in the spirit." (quoted in Bernie S. Siegel, M.D., *Peace, Love, and Healing* [New York: Harper and Row, 1989], p. 227).

Medical science is very well read about the body, but they often overlook the spirit and soul of man. An acquaintance of mine, Nancy Mannies, who is recovering from a brain tumor, has researched this topic extensively. Nancy found that only thirty-four of the 125 medical schools in the United States offer courses in mind and body medicine. These thirty-four include Stanford, UCLA, and Harvard. The connection between the spirit, soul, and body is not something new with the medical field, although some people believe it is a New Age approach. Nancy found that Aristotle (384-322 B.C.) discussed the role of emotions in illness and health at great length. She also found that the Father of medicine, Hippocrates (460-377 B.C.) included the study of the mind as part of the education of his students.

Siegel says that Dr. George Solomon, affiliated with the medicals schools of the University of California in both San Francisco and Los Angeles, published an article entitled "Emotions, Immunity and Disease: A Speculative Theoretical Integration." "When he sent it to me last year, however, next to the word *Speculative* he wrote: 'Not any more'" (Siegel, *Peace, Love, and Healing*, p. 23).

Candace Pert, respected researcher in mind and body medicine, said, "The chemicals that are running our body and our brain are the same chemicals that are involved in emotion. And that says to me that . . . we'd better pay more attention to emotions with respect to health" (Paul E. McGhee, *Health, Healing and the Amuse System* [Dubuque, IA: Kendall/Hunt, 1996], p. 15).

Once again, the Bible teaches it is not body, soul, and spirit, but spirit, soul, and body. I believe that the order of treatment is as important as the treatment itself. The Bible teaches about these three components:

Spirit The Greek word for spirit is *pneuma*. The spirit is the life-giving, invisible, powerful part of man. The spirit was given to man by God. Job 33:4 states, "The Spirit of God has made me; the breath of the Almighty gives me life." Genesis 2:7 tells us, "The Lord God formed the man from the dust of the ground and breathed into his nostrils the breath of life, and the man became a living being." (This is not the same as the Holy Spirit; this is spirit with a small "s.")

Many of the verses in the Bible deal with this spirit. Here are a few:

Luke 8:55: "Her spirit returned, and at once she stood up. Then Jesus told them to give her something to eat."

Acts 7:59 ". . . Stephen prayed, 'Lord Jesus, receive my spirit.'"

Luke 23:46 "Jesus called out with a loud voice, 'Father, into your hands I commit my spirit.'" (See Psalm 31:5.)

James 2:26 "As the body without the spirit is dead, so faith without deeds is dead."

Ecclesiastes 12:7 "and the dust returns to the ground it came from, and the spirit returns to God who gave it."

According to Scripture, the spirit of man can be broken (Job 17:1). It can faint (Ps. 77:3; 142:3; 143:4). The spirit can also fail (Ps. 143:7). Jesus knew this — he was troubled in spirit (John 13:21). This is not uncommon (Dan. 4:19; 7:15). The spirit can be crushed (Ps. 34:18; 38:8; Prov. 15:13,15; 17:22). The spirit is designed to sustain us during times of trouble and trials (Prov. 18:14). But when it is crushed, it cannot do this. When the spirit becomes crushed, physical illness is frequently the resulting outcome.

Signs of a Crushed, Oppressed, or Distressed Spirit

🐾 *loss of confidence:* "So do not throw away your confidence; it will be richly rewarded" (Heb. 10:35).
🐾 *loss of esteem:* "The Lord turned to him and said, 'Go in

the strength you have and save Israel out of Midian's hand. Am I not sending you?' 'But Lord,' Gideon asked, 'how can I save Israel? My clan is the weakest in Manasseh, and I am the least in my family'" (Judg. 6:14-15).

- ⚘ *loss of energy*
- ⚘ *loss of enthusiasm*
- ⚘ *loss of vision and goals:* Solomon wrote, "Where there is no vision, the people perish" (Prov. 29:18, KJV).
- ⚘ *loss of hope:* Solomon wrote, "Hope deferred makes the heart sick, but a longing fulfilled is a tree of life" (Prov. 13:12).

Malachi 3:14-15 states, "You have said, 'It is futile to serve God. What did we gain by carrying out his requirements and going about like mourners before the LORD Almighty? But now we call the arrogant blessed. Certainly the evildoers prosper, and even those who challenge God escape.'"

Medical science recognizes a condition called "Spiritual Distress." It is defined as a "disruption in the life principles that pervades a person's entire being and that integrate and transcend one's biologic and psychosocial nature." Two of the defining characteristics of this condition are

Concern with the meaning of life and death and/or belief systems.

Inner conflict about beliefs, concerns about relationship with deity.

(*Tabor's Cyclopedic Medical Dictionary,* 17th ed. [Philadelphia: F.A. David Company, 1989], pp. 2578-2579.)

This sounds like what Peter went through when he betrayed Jesus:

After a little while, those standing near said to Peter, "Surely you are one of them, for you are a Galilean."

He began to call down curses on himself, and he swore to them, "I don't know this man you're talking about."

Immediately the rooster crowed the second time. Then Peter

remembered the word Jesus had spoken to him: "Before the rooster crows twice you will disown me three times." And he broke down and wept (Mark 14:70-72).

Peter was distressed but repentant in contrast to Judas who suffered such despairing distress of guilt that he hanged himself.

When Judas, who had betrayed him, saw that Jesus was condemned, he was seized with remorse and returned the thirty silver coins to the chief priests and the elders. "I have sinned," he said, "for I have betrayed innocent blood."
"What is that to us?"' they replied. "That's your responsibility."
So Judas threw the money into the temple and left. Then he went away and hanged himself" (Matthew 27:3-5).

Soul (The thoughts, will, and emotions): The soul is the heart of emotions. There are two types of emotions, those which drain and those which fill: negative, life-stealing ones and positive, life-giving ones. Just like a water bed, the soul of man is easier and quicker to drain then it is to fill.

The soul can have many emotions that can hinder and entangle it. Some of them are abandonment, aggression, anger, anxiety, apathy, arrogance, astonishment, bashfulness, boredom, caution, confusion, disappointment, disbelief, discouragement, disenchantment, disgrace, disgust, dispossession, envy, exasperation, exhaustion, fright, frustration, grief, guilt, hatred, horror, humiliation, hurt, misery, obstinance, pain, rage, rejection, remorse, resentment, self-hatred, shame, sorrow, shock, and withdrawal.

These emotions need to be expressed, not suppressed! Supression and denial will eventually intensify emotions. Denied emotions don't die; they only make you sick. This suppression of emotions will usually be expressed by or through the body in several forms. Some common ones are headaches, muscle tension and neck pain. Emotional expressions of suppression may be irritability, irrationality and innappropriate anger expression.

The soul can also have good emotions that reside in it as well. Some of them are boldness, confidence, determination, ecstasy, happiness, joy, love, peace, extroversion, sensitivity, sympathy, sincerity, respect, honor, and thoughtfulness to name a few. The suppression of negative emotions makes it difficult to express positive ones. These positive emotions need to be expressed. When they are not expressed, this can be very stressful.

The Bible has many examples of emotions. A few of the many types of negative emotions found in Psalms that drain the soul of man are listed below:

6:3 — anguish	84:2 — fainting (119:81)
31:7 — affliction, anguish	88:3 — being troubled
31:9 — sorrow, grief	119:20 — overpowering longing
35:12 — feeling forlorn	119:28 — wearisome sorrow
42:5 — feeling downcast (KJV "disquiet")	

Also listed in Psalms are many positive emotions that fill the soul.

25:1 — lifting up my soul (143:8)	86:4 — joy, lifting up my soul
42:1 — panting for God	94:19 — consolation, joy
42:2 — thirsting for God (143:6)	103:1 — praise
42:4 — an outpouring of my soul	130:5-6 — waiting for the Lord
62:1, 5 — finding rest in God	131:2 — stillness and quiet, like a
63:5 — satisfaction	weaned child with its mother
63:8 — clinging to God	146:1 — praise
84:2 — yearning	

The big problem with our thoughts is that they can be taken captive (Col. 2:8). Thoughts determine the course of a person's life (Prov. 4:23). We become what we think about (Prov. 23:7, KJV). Thoughts can be troublesome (Ps. 55:2) as we wrestle with them (Ps. 13:2). These troubling thoughts create stress in our bodies and spirits.

Jesus knew what it was to wrestle with thoughts. He was troubled and distressed by the death of Lazarus even though he knew he would raise Lazarus up (John 11:33, 38). He mourned for the distress of Mary and Martha.

In the Garden of Gethsemane Jesus' thoughts, heart and soul were overwhelmed with sorrow, knowing the burden of agony and sin he was about to bear in the crucifixion (Matthew 26:38).

Stress can have a great control over, and effect on, the mind. There is a natural weakness in the mind because it can easily become overwhelmed and overworked. The Bible teaches that the heart can become faint (Job 23:16; Ps. 61:2; 143:4; Jer. 8:18; Lam. 1:22; 2:11,19; Ezek. 21:7). Faintness of heart can be an outcome of stress in the mind.

Body This is the physical part of man. Jesus said the spirit is willing but the flesh is weak (Matt. 26:41). Many other verses in the Bible speak about the flesh:

Hebrews 2:14: "Since the children have flesh and blood, he too shared in their humanity so that by his death he might destroy him who holds the power of death — that is, the devil."

1 Corinthians 15:50: "I declare to you, brothers, that flesh and blood cannot inherit the kingdom of God, nor does the perishable inherit the imperishable."

John 3:6 "Flesh gives birth to flesh, but the Spirit gives birth to spirit."

Psalm 73:26 "My flesh and my heart may fail, but God is the strength of my heart and my portion forever."

Psalm 78:39 "He remembered that they were but flesh, a passing breeze that does not return."

Psalm 84:2 "My soul yearns, even faints, for the courts of the LORD; my heart and my flesh cry out for the living God."

Psalm 119:120 "My flesh trembles in fear of you; I stand in awe of your laws."

Paul writes in Romans 6:19 that our natural self is weak, and Satan seeks to exploit us. Yet it is true that, as the writer of Hebrews writes, we can become "hindered, encumbered [NASB], and entangled" (12:1). Certainly stress results from those conditions. Paul further writes in 2 Corinthians 7:1, "Since we have these promises, dear friends, let us purify ourselves from everything that contaminates body and spirit, perfecting holiness out of reverence of God." The three parts of man can become contaminated (NIV), filthy (KJV), and defiled (NASB).

These three (spirit, soul and body) or four (wisdom, stature, favor with God, favor with man) areas operate independently as well as dependently. The Bible teaches this concept in several passages.

Several passages show the connection between thoughts and emotions. Daniel is described in the following way in Daniel 4:19: "Then Daniel (also called Belteshazzar) was greatly perplexed for a time, and his thoughts terrified him."

When Jacob was getting ready to be reunited with his brother Esau, he was very worried. He thought his brother would seek to kill him, so he divided his family into groups, thinking, "If Esau comes and attacks one group, the group that is left may escape" (Gen. 32:8). His worry was caused by his thoughts, based on the past.

The connection between spirit and soul is shown in Daniel 7:15: "I, Daniel, was troubled in spirit, and the visions that passed through my mind disturbed me." The effect of thoughts upon the body is seen in Daniel 7:28: "I, Daniel, was deeply troubled by my thoughts, and my face turned pale." Other passages connect stress with physical effects. Joel 2:6 reports, "At the sight of them, nations are in anguish; every face turns pale." Nahum 2:10 states, "She is pillaged, plundered, stripped! Hearts melt, knees give way, bodies tremble, every face grows pale." The stress of shame affects the body in a passage from Isaiah 29:22 which declares, "No longer will Jacob be ashamed; no longer will their faces grow pale."

The connection of soul and body is also seen in Romans 8:5, where "those who live according to the sinful nature [literally, "the flesh"] have their minds set on what that nature desires." The Holy Spirit wants to direct man's spirit and correct this, but man's carnal body and unregenerate mind unite to resist the will of the Spirit. Paul also writes about this conflict in Galatians 5:16-18, "So I say, live by the Spirit, and you will not gratify the desires of the sinful nature. For the sinful nature desires what is contrary to the Spirit, and the Spirit what is contrary to the sinful nature. They are in conflict with each other, so that you do not do what you want. But if you are led by the Spirit, you are not under law." The Holy Spirit and my unconverted human nature (spirit, soul, and body) oppose each other.

Non-Christians are not aware of this conflict because they do not have the indwelling presence of the Holy Spirit. Potentially then, a Christian could have more stress than the non-Christian because of the inner conflict. But Christians have a way of combating stress as they learn to lean upon God and His Spirit.

Consider the following diagram about the three parts of man and how they are related to each other. Look very carefully at the spiritual part of man. Notice that it is divided into two parts. One is the HoS (Holy Spirit). The other is the HuS (Human Spirit).

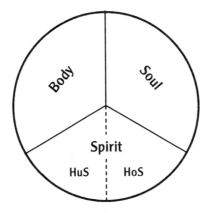

Paul addresses this again in Romans 7:14-20:

We know that the law is spiritual; but I am unspiritual, sold as a slave to sin. I do not understand what I do. For what I want to do I do not do, but what I hate I do. And if I do what I do not want to do, I agree that the law is good. As it is, it is no longer I myself who do it, but it is sin living in me. I know that nothing good lives in me, that is, in my sinful nature. For I have the desire to do what is good, but I cannot carry it out. For what I do is not the good I want to do; no, the evil I do not want to do – this I keep on doing. Now if I do what I do not want to do, it is no longer I who do it, but it is sin living in me that does it.

Paul writes in 2 Corinthians 10:3-5, "For though we live in the world, we do not wage war as the world does. The weapons we fight with are not weapons of the world. On the contrary, they have divine power to demolish strongholds. We demolish arguments and every pretension that sets itself up against the knowledge of God, and we take captive every thought to make it obedient to Christ." The Greek word for strongholds used here is *ochuroma* defined as "fortress." What are these fortresses that Satan tries to develop in a person's soul? What are these thoughts that need to be taken captive to Christ? One area that Satan exploits for his strongholds are our repressed emotions. There appear to be at least four emotions that are easily repressed which inevitably cause stress.

Guilt: Guilt is an emotional torment (2 Cor. 12:7). It makes a person a fugitive (Prov. 28:17). This is because he is afraid that if people really knew him, they would not like him. He is convinced that if his past gets out, he has no present. Guilt and shame drain people of energy and power (Isa. 37:27). People wither and are weakened by guilt.

Guilt creates a great amount of emotional stress (Ezra 9:5-6; 10:9). A guilty mind has a difficult time relaxing, for it is on the defensive. Constant defense is stressful and eventually wears out the body. The guilty wait for people to discover and punish what they have done.

Fear is a very stressful emotion. Genesis 32:7 says that Jacob acted out of "great fear and distress . . . ." Fear is a snare, a trap, and a form of slavery (Prov. 29:25; Heb. 2:15). Satan first learned about fear when he was banished from heaven. He learned how man responds to fear from Adam and Eve in the garden. What he learned from them, he uses against us today.

Fear, when repressed, will only get bigger and more controlling. A fearful person is waiting for the negative events to occur. When good times are happening, the fearful cannot relax because they "know that good times don't last forever." Like guilt, fear puts people on the defensive, draining energy from the body. The physical responses to fear and to stress are nearly the same. Fear, like stress, often hypes up the body, readying it to fight, releasing additional hormones. This rush of hormones is stressful to the body.

Bitterness and anger: Bitterness is an emotion that makes a person "senseless, ignorant, and a brute beast" (Ps. 73:21-22). Bitterness resides in the spirit (Ezek. 3:14; 1 Sam. 30:6) and in the soul (Job 7:11; 10:1). It takes an extreme amount of energy from the body to keep bitterness and anger repressed. This energy is stolen from the immune system, which weakens the body's defenses and makes it susceptible to future illness. Energy stolen to repress bitterness and anger creates further stress.

Inappropriate self-esteem: When we hold too high or too low an opinion of ourselves, we feel either superior or inferior to others. Both conditions are exploited by the devil to his advantage, for both keep our focus off God and on ourselves. Both are very dangerous, for they affect every area of our lives.

These four emotions are often buried so deeply that we are not aware of them and thus do not know that they are creating the stress we feel. Satan loves what these four emotions do to the spirit, soul, and body of the Christian, particularly when they are repressed.

What Are Some of Satan's Goals?

Luke 13:16 - to bind us with physical infirmity
John 10:10 - to kill, steal, and destroy

2 Tim. 2:26 - to capture us to do his will
Heb. 2:14,15 - to enslave us by fear
1 Pet. 5:8 - to devour (Greek: *katapino*, "to drink down")

What Do All Four of These Emotional Strongholds Have in Common?

1. They create physical illness. These are diseases of spirit, soul, and body. They weaken the spirit, soul, and body of man (Job 4:14).

2. They grow with time (Heb. 12:15). A little of these four today will mean more tomorrow.

3. They are burdens, yokes, bondage, and slavery (Rom. 8:15; 2 Tim. 1:7). They become the masters of an individual (2 Pet. 2:19). God wants to free us from these things (John 8:31,32).

4. They come from painful past events (1 Pet. 4:3; Eph. 2:2) and develop as the person dwells on the memory. This stronghold prevents people from enjoying the present and hoping for the future (Isa. 43:18-19; Phil. 3:13).

5. They prevent us from completing the goals God wants from us. They keep us from being what God intends us to be (Num. 13:27-33).

6. They reside in the heart of man. **Guilt** is found in Leviticus 19:17; Job 31:33; Hosea 10:2; **fear** in 2 Samuel 17:10; Psalms 27:3; 112:7,8; Isaiah 21:4; Jeremiah 51;46; **bitterness** in Proverbs 14:10; Jeremiah 4:18; and **inappropriate self-esteem** in Deuteronomy 8;14; Psalm 101:5; Proverbs 16:5; 18:12; Ezekiel 28:5,17; Jeremiah 48:29; 49:16.

7. They are used by Satan to control, influence, and create a heaviness and bondage (Luke 13:16). God says to Ezekiel in 33:10, "Son of man, say to the house of Israel, 'This is what you are saying: "Our offenses and sins weigh us down, and we are wasting away because of them. How then can we live?"'"

8. They wage war against, remove, and destroy the fruit of the Spirit (Rom. 8:5-8).

9. They have related behaviors (Gen. 3:10; Prov. 2:14-15; 21:8). These emotions are roots (Heb. 12:15) that produce a whole crop of behaviors from alcoholism to suicide (Jas. 3:14).

10. They destroy relationships (Col. 3:8,14). The unforgiving spirit which springs from bitterness destroys both parties. But a forgiving spirit actually aids in dealing with stress. In a study of 30 divorced women, Kristy Ashelman from the University of Wisconsin at Madison "found that women who forgave their ex-husbands were less anxious and depressed and became better parents than those who could not forgive" ("Forgiveness—A Healthy Trend" by David Briggs [AP] *The Star Press* [Muncie, IN: December 21, 1997], p. 3A). The article continued: "Other research in recent years has shown people who scored high on forgiveness scales had significantly lower levels of blood pressure, anxiety, and depression, and relatively high self-esteem."

11. They overwhelm us (Ps. 38:4-8; 55:4,5).

What is God's answer for these four strongholds? He wants to deliver us and destroy these emotional strongholds, to remove them from us (Eph. 4:22-24; Col. 3:5-10,15-17). He wants to heal us from these emotions, and he does it by healing from the inside out. Jesus asked the Pharisees, ". . . why are you angry with me for healing the whole man on the Sabbath?" (John 7:23). Healing the whole man means spirit, soul, and body.

Solomon writes in Proverbs 4:23 that the heart needs to be guarded above all else. The reason it should be guarded is that it is the center of a person, the source of all behavior and emotions.

Besides guarding the heart, we must see God and Jesus as possessing these characteristics: Teacher, Lord, Savior, Healer of stronghold emotions. David writes about healing, "Be merciful to me, Lord, for I am faint. O Lord, heal me, for my bones are in agony. My soul is in anguish. How long, O Lord, how long? (Ps.

6:2,3). In another place he writes, "I said, 'O Lord, have mercy on me; heal me, for I have sinned against you'" (Ps. 41:4).

God's Healing Answers for These Specific Strongholds

Guilt: The short term answer is confession (Jas. 5;16). In the long term it is grace resulting in peace (Eph. 2:8,9; Phil. 4:6,7).

Fear: The short term answer is seeking God (Ps. 34:4). In the long term it is faith (Heb. 11:6) and trusting in God (Ps. 56:3; Dan. 6:23; 1 Chr. 5:20).

Bitterness: The short term answer is to bless the people who have hurt you (Matt. 5:44). In the long term it is forgiveness (Matt. 6:14,15; Col. 3:13,14).

Inappropriate Self-esteem: The short term answer is learning from Jesus who you are (Matt. 11:28-30; Eph. 1:3-12). In the long term it is making sure your identity is in Christ (Gal. 2:20).

God's ultimate answer for these strongholds is Jesus. These strongholds are one of the reasons we need a Savior. God wants to become our stronghold (Ps. 9:9; 18:2; 27:1; 144:2).

God's Solution for the Heart

What does God want to do with the heart in which these four emotional strongholds reside?

Jeremiah 24:7 - to give us a heart that knows him.

Jeremiah 31:33 - to write his laws on our hearts.

Jeremiah 32:39 - to give us a singleness of heart.

Ezekiel 11:19 - to give us an undivided heart and a new spirit.

Ezekiel 36:26 - to give us a new heart and spirit.

One of the best wasy to deal with these strongholds is to stop looking at the stronghold and look at God's solution. In Isaiah 32:17-20 God has Isaiah list ten emotional needs people have, characteristics God wants us to have in our hearts. Most of these traits are gifts from God to Christians, gifts which discourage and defeat stress.

Righteousness (17)	Peace (17)
Quietness (17)	Confidence (17)
Peaceful dwelling places (18)	Security (18)
Undisturbed rest (18)	Blessing (20)
Growth potential (20)	Freedom (20)

POINTS TO PONDER

1. How does the devil use guilt as a stronghold? That is, what particular temptations does he put in our way?

2. What is the only good way to deal with guilt? What Scriptures support this answer?

3. Can you think of a time in your life when fear immobilized you? What would you do now if that same situation came up?

4. How does trusting in God keep us from letting Satan use fear to control us?

5. What verses in the Bible help you overcome fear?

6. What does bitterness of spirit do to a person? What is the solution?

7. Read 2 Corinthians 10:12 about comparing yourself with others and relate it to the stronghold of "inappropriate self-esteem."

8. Why is it just as bad to go around feeling inferior as to feel superior? What trap does a sense of being inferior lead to?

9. Reconcile the Scripture which says "Consider others as more important than yourselves" (Phil. 2:4) with the command to "Love your neighbor as yourself" (Matt. 19:19). In what way should we "love" ourselves and in what way should we not?

Chapter 6
THOUGHTS AND
STRESS MANAGEMENT

How and what people think can cause stress. The actions of Jacob illustrate this vividly. Because he thought Esau harbored murderous intentions towards him, he divided his household into two groups. For he thought "if Esau comes and attacks one group, the group that is left may escape" (Gen. 32:7,8). What he thought about Esau caused him such stress that he worried deeply and acted on that worry, causing stress to the whole household.

When confusion takes over, you can be sure of one thing; God is not behind it. "For God is not the author of confusion, but of peace, as in all the churches of the saints" (1 Cor 14:33, KJV). Confusion is undoubtedly one strategy the devil uses to accomplish his goal of separation between us and God. When we allow him to do so, the devil puts thoughts in our minds which revolve endlessly until we are confused and unable to think clearly. You could say we are the victims of "overthinking."

Consider a person who is laid off from a job. That person can see it as an opportunity for getting a better job, as a way of getting an extended vacation, or as financial ruin. The thought he chooses is up to him, but that thought will determine not only the level of stress but also the particular response to the stress. The stressor itself does not cause stress; it is what the person does with it that ends in peace or stress.

Both peace and stress come from the way a person thinks. Paul makes this connection in Philippians 4:7,8. First he talks about a peace that transcends all understanding, and then tells us how we should think: "Whatever is true, whatever is noble, whatever is right, whatever is pure, whatever is lovely, whatever is admirable — if anything is excellent or praiseworthy, think about such things."

Isaiah 60:17 says something amazing — that peace can become our governor. This peace comes only through the Holy Spirit, through allowing him to be the governor of our thought lives

Changing thoughts is probably one of the best ways to get rid of stress. Consider what Abe Lincoln once said about our thought process: "People are about as happy as they make up their minds to be." Phil Mahre (Olympic Gold Medal winner) said, "The most vital aspect of winning is mental attitude." Hans Selye said about stress, "It is not stress that kills us, it is our reaction to it." Look at the following rules:

Rule 1: Don't sweat the small stuff.
Rule 2: It's all small stuff.
Rule 3: If you can't fight or flee, then flow.
Rule 4: It's all a case of mind over matter.
   If you don't mind, it don't matter.
(author unknown)

I remember at Easter time during my childhood I received chocolate bunnies. It was always my hope (an emotion of the soul) these bunnies would be made of solid chocolate. But at times, they were hollow. At times our thoughts are like the bunny, hollow, shallow and empty. These types of thoughts create many problems. This is why Paul tells us not to be taken captive by hollow and deceptive philosophy (Col. 2:8). Instead, Paul writes that our thoughts should be in obedience with the thoughts of Jesus (2 Cor. 10:5). Our thoughts are very important to God. Several Scriptures address this issue.

> Proverbs 4:23 "Above all else, guard your heart, for it is the wellspring of life."

> Proverbs 23:7 "For as he thinketh in his heart, so is he." (KJV).

> Romans 12:2 "Do not conform any longer to the pattern of this world, but be transformed by the renewing of your mind. Then you will be able to test and approve what God's will is — his good, pleasing and perfect will."

> Ephesians 4:23-24 ". . . to be made new in the attitude of your minds; and to put on the new self, created to be like God in true righteousness and holiness."

> Romans 16:19 ". . . but I want you to be wise about what is good, and innocent about what is evil."

> 1 Corinthians 14:20 "Brothers, stop thinking like children. In regard to evil be infants, but in your thinking be adults."

> Matthew 10:16 ". . . Therefore be as shrewed as snakes and as innocent as doves."

The sad thing is that because of our exposure to evil, our thought pattern has become the direct opposite of what God wants. We are very adult when it comes to evil. We know way too much about evil. It comes into our homes through the TV in both sitcoms and news broadcasts. This reversed thought pattern leads to stress and anxiety.

One of the benefits of reading the Bible is that it will help clean out the toxic pollution of our minds. Satan is constantly attacking the mind because it controls a person (Rom. 7:23). This attack is part of his plan of killing, stealing, and destroying (John 10:10). The Holy Spirit, through Paul, said, "We demolish arguments and every pretension that sets itself up against the knowledge of God, and we take captive every thought to make it obedient to Christ" (2 Cor. 10:5). Paul also commands us to have the mind of Christ (Phil. 2:5). Jesus said, "I no longer call you servants, because a servant does not know his master's business. Instead, I have called you friends, for everything that I learned from my Father I have made known to you." (John 15:15). Jesus said later, "I have told you these things, so that in me you may have peace. In this world you will have trouble. But take heart! I have overcome the world" (John 16:33). Certainly the ultimate answer to stress is having the mind of Christ and learning from him.

One of my favorite thoughts about God is that his face shines on us, that God smiles at us. What peace and joy this thought creates! This phrase is found often in the Psalms and is part of a spoken blessing from God to the Israelites in Numbers 6:22-25.

Psalm 4:6-8: "Many are asking, 'Who can show us any good?' Let the light of your face shine upon us, O LORD. You have filled my heart with greater joy than when their grain and new wine abound. I will lie down and sleep in peace. For you alone, O LORD, make me dwell in safety."

Psalm 31:16: "Let your face shine on your servant; save me in your unfailing love.

Psalm 67:1: "May God be gracious to us and bless us and make his face shine upon us."

Psalm 80:3,7,19: "Restore us, O God [Almighty]; make your face shine upon us, that we may be saved."

Psalm 119:135: "Make your face shine upon your servant and teach me your decrees."

Most stress is created by the negative way people think about their situations in life. Thoughts are the foundation on which behavior and life are supported and built (Prov. 23:7, KJV). Some people have built their house on the sand because of the way they think.

What thoughts create stress? If I were to list them all, this book would be huge. Have you heard these before?

☹ I can't do that — it's too difficult.

☹ You can't teach an old dog new tricks.

☹ It's not what you know, it's who you know.

☹ I am a loser.

☹ If it weren't for bad luck, I'd have no luck at all.

☹ I can't forgive myself for what I've done.

☹ I always screw things up.

☹ I knew it was too good to be true.

☹ Nothing ever turns out well.

☹ I am living under a curse.

There are five "nothing" thoughts I hear from people a lot.

☹ I am nothing.

☹ I have nothing.

☹ Nothing good will ever happen to me.

☹ I have accomplished nothing.

☹ I have nothing to offer people in a relationship.

These thoughts are not only self-defeating, they become self-fulfilling. These thoughts can take a bad situation and make it worse, creating the proverbial "mountain out of a mole hill." What should our thoughts be? Philippians 4:8 says it best, "Finally, brothers, whatever is true, whatever is noble, whatever is right, whatever is pure, whatever is lovely, whatever is admirable — if anything is excellent or praiseworthy — think about such things.

King Solomon understood the importance of thoughts. He commands us in Scripture to guard our thoughts because they are the wellspring of life (Prov. 4:23). But how do we do this? The answer lies in Scripture. Psalm 119:9 and 11 give us some of this answer, "How can a young man keep his way pure? By living according to your word"; "I have hidden your word in my heart that I might not sin against you."

One of the best ways to get rid of stress is through one of the oldest disciplines in the world — meditation. The sad thing is that this discipline is frequently the most overlooked in the Christian lifestyle. Meditation means to contemplate and reflect on the Word of God. In Psalm 1:1a-2 David writes, "Blessed is the man . . . [whose] delight is in the law of the LORD, and on his law he meditates day and night."

Joshua 1:8 commands meditation, "Do not let this Book of the Law depart from your mouth; meditate on it day and night, so that you may be careful to do everything written in it. Then you will be prosperous and successful." Jeremiah 15:16 talks about Jeremiah's attitude toward the word of God, "When your words came, I ate them; they were my joy and my heart's delight. . . ." David writes in Psalm 119:72, "The law from your mouth is more precious to me than thousands of pieces of silver and gold." Psalm 119:103: "How sweet are your words to my taste, sweeter than honey to my mouth!"

There are many things on which Christians should meditate. One of the best is God's unfailing love. Jeremiah wrote, "Because of the LORD's great love we are not consumed, for his compassions never fail. They are new every morning; great is your faithfulness" (Lam. 3:22-23). Psalm 48:9 gives the following directive, "Within your temple, O God, we meditate on your unfailing love." What a great thing to meditate on. Not that we love God, but that God loves us! The word "unfailing" means "never failing." God's love for us will **never** fail.

The word "unfailing" is found in the New International Version of the Bible 35 times. In all but three of these times "love" is in these passages. Most of these passages are found in the Psalms. Some of the ones I really like are

13:5 — "But I trust in your unfailing love; my heart rejoices in your salvation."

32:10 — "Many are the woes of the wicked, but the LORD's unfailing love surrounds the man who trusts in him."

33:5 — "The LORD loves righteousness and justice; the earth is full of his unfailing love."

33:22 — "May your unfailing love rest upon us, O LORD, even as we put our hope in you."

44:26 — "Rise up and help us; redeem us because of your unfailing love."

85:7 — "Show us your unfailing love, O LORD, and grant us your salvation."

119:41 — "May your unfailing love come to me, O LORD, your salvation according to your promise."

119:76 — "May your unfailing love be my comfort, according to your promise to your servant."

130:7 — "O Israel, put your hope in the LORD, for with the LORD is unfailing love and with him is full redemption."

147:11 — "The LORD delights in those who fear him, who put their hope in his unfailing love."

A great stress-reducing thought is that there is nothing we can do that would cause God to love us more or less than he does right now. This thought should bring peace and rest. Paul wrote to the Church at Ephesus, ". . . And I pray that you, being rooted and established in love, may have power, together with all the saints, to grasp how wide and long and high and deep is the love of Christ, and to know this love that surpasses knowledge — that you may be filled to the measure of all the fullness of God" (Eph. 3:17-19).

Paul writes through the Holy Spirit to the people at Rome, "For I am convinced that neither death nor life, neither angels nor demons, neither the present nor the future, nor any powers, neither height nor depth, nor anything else in all creation, will be able to separate us from the love of God that is in Christ Jesus our Lord (Rom. 8:38-39).

Paul writes to the Church at Ephesus, "But because of his great love for us, God, who is rich in mercy, made us alive with Christ even when we were dead in transgressions — it is by grace you have been saved (Eph. 2:4-5). These are two great passages to meditate on that will help overcome stress.

Meditating on God's faithfulness to his people is also a

great way of reducing and eliminating stress. Several Psalms deal with God's faithfulness.

57:3 — "He sends from heaven and saves me, rebuking those who hotly pursue me; God sends his love and his faithfulness."

57:9-10 — "I will praise you, O Lord, among the nations; I will sing of you among the peoples. For great is your love, reaching to the heavens; your faithfulness reaches to the skies."

89:5 — "The heavens praise your wonders, O Lord, your faithfulness too, in the assembly of the holy ones."

89:8 — "O Lord God Almighty, who is like you? You are mighty, O Lord, and your faithfulness surrounds you."

89:14 — "Righteousness and justice are the foundation of your throne; love and faithfulness go before you."

91:4 — "He will cover you with his feathers, and under his wings you will find refuge; his faithfulness will be your shield and rampart."

92:2 — "To proclaim your love in the morning and your faithfulness at night."

98:3 — "He has remembered his love and his faithfulness to the house of Israel; all the ends of the earth have seen the salvation of our God."

100:5 — "For the Lord is good and his love endures forever; his faithfulness continues through all generations."

108:4 — "For great is your love, higher than the heavens; your faithfulness reaches to the skies."

117:2 — "For great is his love toward us, and the faithfulness of the Lord endures forever."

119:90 — "Your faithfulness continues through all generations; you established the earth, and it endures."

Meditating on the comfort of God also has a benefit of reducing stress.

Psalm 23:4 — ". . . I will fear no evil, for you are with me; your rod and your staff, they comfort me."

71:21 — "You will increase my honor and comfort me once again."

119:50 — "My comfort in my suffering is this: Your promise preserves my life." Dwelling on God's promises is a wonderful way of reducing stress.

119:52 — "I remember your ancient laws, O LORD, and I find comfort in them." This passage also makes a connection with remembering God's laws as a way of finding comfort.

119:76 — "May your unfailing love be my comfort, according to your promise to your servant." This passage also makes a link with dwelling on the unfailing love of God!

Psalms also teaches us to meditate on God's works (77:12; 143:5); God's precepts, decrees and statutes (119:15,23,48,78, 99); God's wonders (119:27); God's promises (119:148); and God's wonderful works (145:5).

Another way to deal with stress is to memorize Scripture. This is a great defense against the universe of stress in which our planet moves. Scripture is a sword against stress (Eph. 6:17). Memorizing Scripture makes it a weapon in destroying the emotions and thoughts that create stress. Jesus said in Matthew 4:4, "Man does not live on bread alone, but on every word that comes from the mouth of God." One of my favorite passages to memorize and visualize is Psalm 23. The words highlighted are the ones I want you to dwell on.

(Vs 1) "The LORD is **my shepherd**": I am God's sheep (Ps. 100:3). By the way, this is not a compliment. Chuck Swindoll said on the February 24, 1998 *Insight for Living* program that you don't see trained sheep in the circus because they are dumb animals. I was recently told by a person who raised sheep that they will eat weeds instead of grass, and frequently after giving birth to their young, the mother will leave the lamb by itself. Being human proves we need a shepherd — a good one (John 10:11; Heb. 13:20; Rev. 7:17).

(Vs 1) **"I shall not be in want"**: He meets all my needs (Phil. 4:19).

(Vs 2) **"He makes me** lie down in **green pasture"s**: He puts me in lush places (Jer. 33:12). Psalm 4:8 promises, "I will lie down and sleep in peace, for you alone, O LORD, make me dwell in safety."

(Vs 2) **"He leads me** beside **quiet waters"**: He knows my fears, so he takes me to quiet places (Isa. 40:11; Ezek. 34:14; Rev. 7:17).

(Vs 3) **"He restores** my soul"**: He builds me back up by his presence in my life and by his word (Ps. 19:7; 147:2; Isa. 38:16).

(Vs 3) **"He guides** me in paths of righteousness for his name's sake"**: He leads me in my path of life (Ps. 5:8; 67:4; 85:13).

(Vs 4) **"Even though I walk through** the valley of the shadow of death"**: I am going to go through many troubles (John 16:33).

(Vs 4) "I will fear no evil, for **you are with me**"**: I should not fear the valleys because God is with me at all times, in all places (Deut. 31:6,8; Isa. 43:2).

(Vs 4) "Your rod and your staff, they **comfort me**"**: God gives me things to comfort me (Isa. 40:1).

(Vs 5) **"You prepare** a table before me in the presence of my enemies"**: God has prepared many good things for me (Ps. 103:5; John 14:2; 1 Cor. 2:9-10).

(Vs 5) **"You anoint** [Ps. 92:10] my head with oil; **my cup overflows** [Ps. 16:5]"**: So many good things that I cannot hold them all (1 Cor. 1:5; Prov. 3:10).

(Vs 6) **"Surely goodness and love will follow me all the days of**

my life, and I will dwell in the house of the LORD forever": Good things are ahead in my life. I will dwell with God for the rest of eternity (Ps. 25:7; 84:11; 21:3-4).

By meditating on the highlighted words and the verses after them, peace is a supernatural, God-given result. Keep focusing on this passage on a daily basis. Psalm 107:20 says, "He sent for his word and healed them; he rescued them from the grave."

Not only is memorization of Scripture a great way of defeating stress but so is *obeying* Scripture. James taught that we should not merely listen to the word, but we should do what it says (Jas. 1:22). Jesus said, "Therefore everyone who hears these words of mine and puts them into practice is like a wise man who built his house on the rock. The rain came down, the streams rose, and the winds blew and beat against that house; yet it did not fall, because it had its foundation on the rock" (Matt. 7:24-25).

Here are ten thoughts on which I encourage you to meditate. These thoughts are the ten "P"s to believe for emotional stability and spiritual mental health. As Christians:

- ℘ God is *pleased* with you (Eph. 1:5; 2 Cor. 2:15).
- ℘ God's *presence* is with you (Ps. 23:4; 121:7-8; Matthew 28:20).
- ℘ Your life is a *presentation* to God (Matt. 5:14-16; Rom. 12:1-2).
- ℘ God has given you *power* (Eph. 1:18-20). Paul writes to the church at Ephesus, "Now to him who is able to do immeasurably more than all we ask or imagine, according to his power that is at work within us, to him be glory in the church and in Christ Jesus throughout all generations, for ever and ever! Amen" (Eph. 3:20-21).
- ℘ God has given you *purpose* (Ps. 138:8; Eph. 1:12).
- ℘ You are *precious* to God (Ps. 116:15; Eph. 1:4; 1 Pet. 1:3)
- ℘ God has given you his *promises* (2 Pet. 1:3-4; 2 Cor. 1:20).
- ℘ God has *purchased* you (Ps. 74:2; 1 Cor. 6:18-19).
- ℘ God will *provide* for you (1 Tim. 6:17; 1 Pet. 4:11).

℘ You are at **peace** with God. Ephesians 2:14-15 assures us, "For he himself is our peace, who has made the two one and has destroyed the barrier, the dividing wall of hostility, by abolishing in his flesh the law with its commandments and regulations. His purpose was to create in himself one new man out of the two, thus making peace."

How many of these ten thoughts do you believe? How many do you not believe? What makes these thoughts so difficult to believe? One of the things that makes them difficult to believe is that they are all positive. As human beings, we tend to believe the negative over the positive. We tend to think that criticism is more truthful than compliments. This type of thought pattern really creates stress. Let me close with some thoughts about God you should think on, especially during stress. Four come to mind:

➤ God has not forgotten you and your situations (Heb. 13:5-6).
➤ God has not forsaken you (1 John 3:1).
➤ God has not left you (Matt. 28:19-20; John 14:18; 1 John 4:4).
➤ God has not rejected you (1 John 4:9-10).

When we believe the opposite of these thoughts (which is Satan's goal), stress increases and a bad situation appears worse than it is.

Points to Ponder

1. Do you really believe God is pleased with you? Why or why not? Read Ephesians 1:5 and 2 Corinthians 2:15 and answer again.

2. What does it mean to have God's presence with us at all times? Are there times we wish he were somewhere else? Times when he does not seem near? What do we hold on to at those times?

3. What are some ways to use the power God has given, as proclaimed in Ephesians 1:18-20 and 3: 20-21?

4. How does knowing you have purpose affect your life?

5. Do you know that you are precious in God's sight? How does that knowledge affect your decisions?

6. List some of God's promises which help you deal with stress.

7. Why did God need to purchase us? What do you do differently as a result?

8. Tell of an incident which showed you that God will provide for you.

Chapter 8
JOY AND STRESS:
LAUGHTER IS THE BEST MEDICINE.

One of my favorite books in the Bible is the book of Philippians. The reason I like it is because the theme is joy. Paul wrote this letter around A.D. 61, while in jail. The word joy and its various derivatives occur sixteen times. The breakdown is "joy" (Greek *chara*) 5 times; "rejoice" (Greek *chairein*) 9 times; and "shared joy" (Greek *synchairein*) 2 times. This letter does not deal with joy brought about by good times, but rather joy forged from hardships.

Chara and *chairein* mean an attitude of internal joy and delight. This word is found several times in the New Testament. Jesus spoke many times about joy. Many of these times are found in the parables.

✸ Matthew 13:44-46 — "The kingdom of heaven is like treasure hidden in a field. When a man found it, he hid it again, and then in his joy went and sold all he had and bought that field. Again, the kindom of heaven is like a merchant looking for fine pearls. When he found one of great value, he went away and sold everything he had and bought it."

✸ Luke 15:5-6 — "And when he finds it, he joyfully puts it on his shoulders and goes home. Then he calls his friends and neighbors together and says, 'Rejoice with me; I have found my lost sheep.'"

✯ Luke 15:32 — "But we had to celebrate and be glad, because this brother of yours was dead and is alive again; he was lost and is found."

The Bible speaks about joy in all types of trials and triumphs. The Bible speaks of joy in hard times (Jas. 1:2). The Bible also speaks of joy in positive events. Look at these verses:

Acts 8:5-8 — "Philip went down to a city in Samaria and proclaimed the Christ there. When the crowds heard Philip and saw the miraculous signs he did, they all paid close attention to what he said. With shrieks, evil spirits came out of many, and many paralytics and cripples were healed. So there was great joy in that city."

Acts 8:39 — "When they came out of the water, the Spirit of the Lord suddenly took Philip away, and the eunuch did not see him again, but went on his way rejoicing." (See also Acts13:48.)

1 Thessalonians 3:9 — "How can we thank God enough for you in return for all the joy we have in the presence of our God because of you?"

Romans 16:19 — ". . . I am full of joy over you . . ."

The Bible also addresses joy with suffering and persecution. These verses express this:

Matthew 5:11-12 — "Blessed are you when people insult you, persecute you and falsely say all kinds of evil against you because of me. Rejoice and be glad, because great is your reward in heaven, for in the same way they persecuted the prophets who were before you."

Acts 5:41 — "The apostles left the Sanhedrin, rejoicing because they had been counted worthy of suffering disgrace for the Name."

Colossians 1:11-12 — "being strengthened with all power

according to his glorious might so that you may have great endurance and patience, and joyfully giving thanks to the Father, who has qualified you to share in the inheritance of the saints in the kingdom of light."

1 Peter 4:13 — "But rejoice that you participate in the sufferings of Christ, so that you may be overjoyed when his glory is revealed."

My favorite verse about joy in the Old Testament is Nehemiah 8:10. It assures us that "the joy of the LORD is your strength."

Leviticus 23:40 commands the Israelites,"On the first day you are to take choice fruit from the trees, and palm fronds, leafy branches and poplars, and rejoice before the LORD your God for seven days."

Deuteronomy 12:7 states, "There, in the presence of the LORD your God, you and your families shall eat and shall rejoice in everything you have put your hand to, because the LORD your God has blessed you."

Deuteronomy 12:18 reiterates, "Instead, you are to eat them in the presence of the LORD your God at the place the LORD your God will choose — you, your sons and daughters, your menservants and maidservants, and the Levites from your towns — and you are to rejoice before the LORD your God in everything you put your hand to."

Other verses about rejoicing that I like are Deuteronomy 16:11, 14-15; Isaiah 61:10; 25:9; 35:2,10.

My favorite verse in Philippians is 3:1, which reads, "Finally, my brothers, rejoice in the Lord! It is no trouble for me to write the same things to you again, and it is a *safeguard* for you." The reason I like this verse is because of the highlighted word — safeguard. The Greek adjective here is *asphales* meaning "certain, secure, safe." Rejoicing is a safeguard against things that stress people out.

Probably the most famous verse in Philippians is 4:4, which

says, "Rejoice in the Lord always. I will say it again: Rejoice!" Don't forget where Paul was when he wrote this — prison. Philippians is one of the four prison letters Paul wrote. Colossians, Ephesians and Philemon are the other three (Phil. 1:7,17; Eph. 6:20; Col. 4:18; Phlm. 1:1). As Paul would say, joy then does not come from place but from an attitude of the heart. He is writing not only to the Church at Philippi, but to us and even himself. I am sure that his rejoicing kept him from "losing his mind" while he was incarcerated.

There are three nouns in the Greek used for the word joy in the New Testament:

Chara — joy, delight (Mark 4:16)
Agalliasis — exultation; exuberant joy (Luke 1:44)
Euphrosyne — joy (Acts 2:28)

There are four verbs in the Greek used for joy in the New Testament:

Chairo — to rejoice; to be glad (Phil. 1:18)
Kauchaomai — to boast, glory, exult (Romans 5:11)
Agalliao — to exult, to rejoice greatly (John 8:56)
Euphraino to cheer, gladden (Rom. 15:10)

According to the Bible rejoicing comes from five things:
Heart — 1 Chronicles 16:10; Psalm 33:21
Soul — Psalm 35:9
Spirit — Luke 1:47
Earth — Psalm 97:1
God's people — Psalm 118:24

A mind-set that rejoices is a great deterrent against becoming stressed out. This mind-set is also a discipline! It is a combination of two of the fruits of the Spirit — joy and self-control (Gal. 5:22-23). When the mind-set does not look for the joyful side of situations, it not only invites stress into the heart, it also creates it! Paul in Romans 8:5 spoke about this, "Those who live according to the sinful nature have their mind set on what that nature desires; but those who live in accordance with the Spirit have their minds set on what the Spirit desires."

The mind-set that is with the Spirit brings peace, which is a gift from God to help us deal with stressful times and events. Peace of mind does not calm down the stressor, but it sure calms the stressee. I believe that this peace only comes from three sources:

God: Romans 1:7; 1 Corinthians 1:3; 2 Corinthians 1:2; Ephesians 1:2; Philippians 1:2; 4:7; Colossians 1:2; 1 Thessalonians 1:1; 2 Thessalonians 1:1; 1 Timothy 1:2; Philemon 3

Christ: John 14:27; Colossians 3:15

Holy Spirit: Galatians 5:22

One of the best passages on rejoicing is found in Habakkuk 3:17-19:

> Though the fig tree does not bud and there are no grapes on the vines, though the olive crop fails and the fields produce no food, though there are no sheep in the pen and no cattle in the stalls, yet I will rejoice in the LORD, I will be joyful in God my Savior. The Sovereign LORD is my strength; he makes my feet like the feet of a deer, he enables me to go on the heights.

What a powerful verse on rejoicing during stressful times. What a powerful verse on the results of rejoicing during stressful times — ". . . he makes my feet like the feet of a deer, he enables me to go on the heights."

Joy and rejoicing are addressed frequently in Psalms:

2:11 — "Serve the LORD with fear and rejoice with trembling."

4:7 — "You have filled my heart with greater joy than when their grain and new wine abound."

5:11 — ". . . that those who love your name may rejoice in you."

9:14 — "that I may declare your praises in the gates of the Daughter of Zion and there rejoice in your salvation."

51:8 — "Let me hear joy and gladness; let the bones you have crushed rejoice."

68:3 — "But may the righteous be glad and rejoice before God; may they be happy and joyful."

89:16 — "They rejoice in your name all day long; they exult in your righteousness."

96:11-13 — "Let the heavens rejoice, let the earth be glad; let the sea resound, and all that is in it; let the fields be jubilant, and everything in them. Then all the trees of the forest will sing for joy; they will sing before the LORD, for he comes, he comes to judge the earth. He will judge the world in righteousness and the peoples in his truth."

97:1 — "The LORD reigns, let the earth be glad; let the distant shores rejoice."

149:2 — "Let Israel rejoice in their Maker; let the people of Zion be glad in their King. Let them praise his name with dancing and make music to him with tambourine and harp."

Psalm 150 mentions the word "praise" 13 times. This psalm teaches that people should praise God for:
- his acts of power (2)
- his greatness (2)

It also teaches that people should praise God with:
- trumpets, harp, and lyre (3)
- tambourine, dancing, strings, and flute (4)
- cymbals (5)

The last verse in Psalm 150 says it best and says it all, "Let everything that has breath praise the LORD. Praise the LORD."

Laughter and Stress Reduction and Management

Laughter is a great way to deal with stress. I have been teaching a stress management class to cardiac patients at the local hospital for the past five years. One of my goals in this class is to help people learn to laugh and laugh more often.

This might surprise you, but Sigmund Freud might have been the first psychologist to show that laughter can defeat stress. In 1916 he wrote a book called *Wit and Its Relation to the Unconscious* (New York: Moffat Yard). Martin Grotjahn said, "A wit is an angry man in search of a victim. A witticism is his way of releasing repressed hostility. . . . Laughter, as it provides a permissible release of unconscious aggressions, is one of the best safeguards of mental health" (Karl Menninger, *The Vital Balance*, p. 137). In other words, laughter is good for stress management!

Solomon wrote, "There is a time for everything, and a season for every activity under heaven." He also wrote, "a time to weep and a time to laugh, a time to mourn and a time to dance" (Eccl. 3:1,4). Laughter is one of the best medications (Prov. 17:22) this world has ever known. It is a medication for the spirit, soul and body of man. It costs nothing, but what it does is priceless.

Laughter is a gift from God for man that can lift and heal the soul and spirit. We are the only creature invented by God that can laugh. Laughter is a gift that has unlimited healing potential. Red Skelton said, "No matter what your heartache may be, laughing helps you forget it for a few seconds." Viktor Frankl, a psychiatrist who was placed in a Nazi concentration camp in World War II, wrote a book titled *Man's Search for Meaning*. He said, "I would never have made it if I could not have laughed. Laughing lifted me momentarily . . . out of this horrible situation, just enough to make it livable . . . survivable" (McGhee, *Amuse*, p. 34).

Norman Cousins understood the healing power of laughter. In 1964 he contracted a fatal connective tissue disease. Traditional medicine did not stop the illness. On his own, he used laughter and courage and high doses of vitamin C to conquer this illness. Cousins found out that ten minutes of laughter would give him two hours of sleep without pain. He wrote a book about what he learned titled *Anatomy of an Illness* (New York: Bantam, 1979). I guess Proverbs 17:22 is right, laughter *is* the best medicine.

Dr. Raymond A. Moody said, "Over the years, I have encountered a surprising number of instances in which, to all appearances, patients have laughed themselves back to health, or at least have used their sense of humor as a very positive and adaptive response to their illness" (McGhee, *Amuse*, p. 3).

Too many times, in times of stress, laughter is quickly lost. In recent years much research has been done on the topic of laughter, stress and healing. Research has shown that laughter does a variety of very positive things for the spirit, soul, and body of man. Some of this research suggests that laughter has many benefits.

Muscular Benefits of Laughter:

✧ Strengthens heart muscles.

✧ Helps to move nutrients and oxygen to body tissues

✧ Increases the production of endorphins in the body. This chemical is an opiate-like substance — the body's own natural painkiller. Research has shown that endorphins are 20 to 30 times more potent than morphine (Maxine L. Patrick, et al., *Medical-Surgical Nursing* [Philadephia: J.B. Lippincott, 1986], p. 94).

✧ Increases production of certain chemicals from glands of the body (adrenal, hypothalamus and pituitary).

✧ Relaxes muscles as they constrict and relax throughout the entire body.

✧ Increases immune cells that fight disease.

✧ Reduces four stress hormones, epinephrine, cortisol, dopac and growth hormone. (From L.S. Berk, et al., "Neuroendocrine and stress hormone changes during mirthful laughter," *American Journal of Medical Sciences* [1989]: 298, 390-396).

✧ Increases the body's natural painkiller cells. Groucho Marx said, "A clown is like an aspirin, only he works twice as fast."

The Psychological Benefits of Laughter:

✧ Extinguishes body tension.
✧ Gives a psychological boost.
✧ Reduces stress.

Cardiovascular Benefits of Laughter:

✧ Decreases blood pressure.
✧ Increases the heart rate short term, pumping more blood throughout the body.
✧ Lowers heart rate long term. It is believed that laughter actually puts blood pressure in manageable limits.
✧ Enhances circulation

It appears that what stress does to the body negatively, laughter reverses to the positive. As I close this book, I want to close with a quote from Bob Hope. "I have seen what a laugh can do. It can transform almost unbearable tears into something bearable, even hopeful" (McGhee, *Amuse*, p. 191). Let me give you a new life goal. The goal should be to get more laughter injected into your life. I am convinced that if you would laugh four hours a week, (which is $\frac{1}{42}$ of your week), you would not only extend your life expectancy, but also enhance your lifestyle.

POINTS TO PONDER

1. Why do Christians not laugh more? About what do we have to rejoice?

2. Is joy always expressed in laughter? Why or why not?

3. Are there some things about which we should not laugh? List some (Eph. 5:1-4).

4. Are there things we should not rejoice in, according to 1 Corinthians 13:6 and Romans 12:15?

5. How is a person able to rejoice in adversity? Read James 1:3,4; Romans 5:3-5.

Appendix
31 Days to Overcoming Stress

Practice these things until they become a habit. It may take awhile for them to become a pattern in your life.

1. *Follow an unconventional schedule.* If possible, go to work at a time when the traffic isn't heavy. Watch your speed; take the slow, scenic route if you can. Getting out of the routine will give you a simple way to manage stress.

2. *Don't compare yourself to others.* Paul writes in Galatians 6:4, "Each one should test his own actions. Then he can take pride in himself, without comparing himself to somebody else." Comparison is not healthy. It creates mental and emotional stress. When you compare yourself with others, you feel either inferior or superior to them and neither attitude is healthy.

Comparison lends itself to becoming hypercritical of yourself. This leads to anger which is the worst kind of stress. One of the best ways to deal with this is to stop all self-criticism. I frequently ask my clients to set this goal for themselves: no words of disrespect or "put-down" of self are allowed; only genuine compliments are spoken of and to oneself. Many people have a difficult time doing this.

One of the most stressful comparisons people make is comparing themselves to their younger selves. When I was 20 I did not require as much sleep as I do now. I frequently went to bed past midnight. I had an abundance of energy: I could run several miles a day. But last year I turned 40, and what I could do 20 years ago, I can't do now. I don't have the energy or strength for it. The truth is I don't even want to do what I did 20 years ago.

Along with this point of comparison, people often build their self-esteem on their accomplishments or possessions. Do not think of yourself as equal to what you do or have; you are valuable for who you are as a person.

3. *Exercise on a regular basis.* Know what your body limits are with exercise. The old statement, "No pain, no gain" is not true nor is it wise. Choose an exercise that you enjoy doing. I read an article that said the first exercise we learned to do is probably the best. What is this exercise? Walking — one of the cheapest exercises in the world and one of the simplest. You may not have thought about the fact that Jesus must have been in great shape. Think about it — he walked everywhere he went (Luke 24:15). We can follow his example by walking as much as is reasonable for us

An article titled, "Walking Away from a Heart Attack" (*Walking Magazine*, Sept./Oct. 1993) said that walking can help control blood pressure and arrhythmias (irregular heartbeats). The article also stated that walking is good for weight loss and management, and raising high-density lipoproteins ("good" cholesterol). This good cholesterol is protection against heart disease. In *The Journal of the American Medical Association* (February 18, 1998) there was an article about a study that showed walking six times a month for a half-hour each time appears to lower the rate of premature death by 44 percent.

You should get your heart rate up and sweat when you are exercising. I call this "pops" (point of perspiration). Our bodies need to sweat, for this is one of the ways our body rids itself of stress. By the way, muscle is the only substance I know of that the more you use it, the stronger it gets.

4. *Don't overschedule your day.* If at all possible, don't let others do your scheduling. Work from a list of priorities and don't procrastinate. Be good to yourself and work a schedule that gives you plenty of time to relax and enjoy life. Remember that when you're not at work, you're not at work. When you can, don't wear a watch. This is especially true when you are on vacation, or when you are home after work. The simple act of removing your watch can help you relax and enjoy time, not measure and monitor it.

5. *Learn to get away and relax without feeling guilty.* Relaxation is not doing nothing. It is doing something very positive for your body. Fifteen minutes of relaxation a day is a great way to reduce stress; you might use the time to pray and unwind. Relaxation on a regular basis has been known to decrease anxiety and blood pressure while boosting the immune system, reversing heart disease, improving stamina and judgment. (*Working Woman* [May 18, 1993], pp. 83-84, 100-101).

One of the most stressful times in Jesus' ministry had to be when he learned of the beheading of his cousin John the Baptist. After this event, Jesus withdrew to a solitary place. Matthew 14:22-23 says of Jesus, "Immediately Jesus made the disciples get into the boat and go on ahead of him to the other side, while he dismissed the crowd. After he had dismissed them, he went up on a mountainside by himself to pray. When evening came, he was there alone."

On other occasions Jesus left the crowds and went to a quiet place to pray. Mark 1:35 tells us, "Very early in the morning, while it was still dark, Jesus got up, left the house and went off to a solitary place, where he prayed." Luke 5:16 says about Jesus, "Jesus often withdrew to lonely places and prayed."

Silence is important during this time of relaxation. It is valuable to get away from all the noise and stress and find a quiet place to give you some quiet time. Wayne Oates says, "Silence is not native to my world. Silence, more than likely, is a stranger to your world, too. If you and I ever have silence in our noisy hearts, we are going to have to grow it. . . . You can nurture silence in your noisy heart if you value it, cherish it, and are eager to nourish it" (Wayne E. Oates, *Nurturing Silence in a Noisy Heart* [Garden City, NY: Doubleday, 1979], p. 3).

6. *Have music on during your day.* In 1 Samuel 18:10 we read, "The next day an evil [injurious] spirit from God came forcefully upon Saul. He was prophesying in his house, while David was playing the harp, as he usually did." David played the harp to soothe and get rid of Saul's stress.

Music is a great way to reduce stress and anxiety, but it must be music that you like. Music styles that you dislike tend to hype you up. Hymns that we have sung for years can reduce our stress. Two in particular come to mind. The first one is "Does Jesus Care?" by Frank E. Graeff, 1901. My favorite words in this song are:

> Does Jesus care when my heart is pained
> Too deeply for mirth and song;
> As the burdens press, and the cares distress,
> And the way grows weary and long?
> Oh yes, He cares; I know He cares,
> His heart is touched with my grief;
> When the days are weary, the long nights dreary,
> I know my Savior cares.

The second song I love is "This Is My Father's World" by Maltbie D. Babcock, 1901. The words I like in this song say:

> This is my Father's world:
> I rest me in the thought
> Of rocks and trees, of skies and seas;
> His hand the wonders wrought.
> This is my Father's world;

Why should my heart be sad?
The Lord is King; let the heavens ring!
God reigns: let earth be glad.

1901 must have been a good year. Both of these hymns were written back then, but they are more significant today as stress mounts and faith falls. I would encourage you to visualize them as you sing them. Visualize that Jesus cares and that this is *my* Father's world.

A verse about singing that fascinates me is Zephaniah 3:17 which reads, "The LORD your God is with you, he is mighty to save. He will take great delight in you, he will quiet you with his love, he will rejoice over you with singing." What a great thing to meditate on — God sings over us and he will quiet us with his love! Visualizing the actions in this verse brings peace to the heart in stressful times. I picture God singing over us like a parent singing a young child to sleep.

It is not surprising that the psalms speak about singing because the book of Psalms was the hymnal of the people then. Some of the sing(ing) verses in Psalms that I really like are the following:

18:49: "Therefore I will praise you among the nations, O LORD; I will sing praises to your name."

100:2 "Worship the LORD with gladness; come before him with joyful songs."

126:2 "Our mouths were filled with laughter, our tongues with songs of joy. Then it was said among the nations, 'The LORD has done great things for them.'"

In the past several years, Christian music and radio have been on the increase. In Central Indiana where I live, five years ago we had no Christian radio in our area. Today, I am glad to say that there are three Christian radio stations. Listening to this music brings peace to the soul.

7. *Have good friends with which to share troubles.* In Hebrews it says, "And do not forget to do good and to share with others, for with such sacrifices God is pleased" (Heb. 13:16). Paul writes, "Carry each other's burdens, and in this way you fulfill the law of Christ" (Gal. 6:2). He also writes, "Let us not become weary in doing good, for at the proper time we will reap a harvest if we do not give up. Therefore, as we have opportunity, let us do good to all people, especially to those who belong to the family of believers" (Gal. 6:9-10).

Moses understood this concept after Jethro suggested it. Jethro was Moses' father-in-law. When he saw how Moses was governing the people daily, he said to him:

> What you are doing is not good. You and these people who come to you will only wear yourselves out. The work is too heavy for you; you cannot handle it alone. Listen now to me and I will give you some advice, and may God be with you. You must be the people's representative before God and bring their disputes to him. Teach them the decrees and laws, and show them the way to live and the duties they are to perform. But select capable men from all the people — men who fear God, trustworthy men who hate dishonest gain — and appoint them as officials over thousands, hundreds, fifties and tens. Have them serve as judges for the people at all times, but have them bring every difficult case to you; the simple cases they can decide themselves. That will make your load lighter, because they will share it with you. If you do this and God so commands, you will be able to stand the strain, and all these people will go home satisfied. Moses listened to his father-in-law and did everything he said (Exod. 18:17-24).

All of us need people we can rely on when we need help. If you look at the life of Jesus, you will find that he was closer to Peter, James, and John, and he shared more with them than the other disciples; these three disciples were also with him at the Mount of Transfiguration (Matt. 17:1). He shared with them the stress he was feeling when he was in the garden of Gethsemane (Matt. 26:37-38).

I would encourage you to do four things with your support people:

    a. Give yourself permission to be truthful with them about what is going on in your life.

    b. Meet on a regular basis.

    c. Share your weaknesses with them. Paul wrote in Galatians 6:2 to carry each other's burdens — allow people to help you carry your burdens.

    d. Pray regularly for and with them.

You are developing your "stress team." The advantage of this approach is that in a team

Together
Everyone
Accomplishes
More

This stress team approach creates "synergy." Synergy is this principle: what two can accomplish together is greater than what they can accomplish alone. Some of the benefits follow:

There is power and strength in numbers.

More accomplished in less time.

Less stress because you have a person supporting, harmonizing with, and encouraging you.

Work is more fun when done together.

It's not you against the world.

Paul understood this concept when he wrote, "But God, who comforts the downcast, comforted us by the coming of Titus, and not only by his coming but also by the comfort you had given him. He told us about your longing for me, your deep sorrow, your ardent concern for me, so that my joy was greater than ever" (2 Cor. 7:6-7). Knowing that people are concerned about you and that they care for you reduces stress.

The Bible has many warnings about people with whom you should not associate (Prov. 13:20; 22:24,25). Paul writes in 1 Corinthians 15:33 that "bad company corrupts good character."

While caring hands can reduce stress, uncaring people can cause extremely stressful conditions. If you are around "drainers and complainers," you know what I mean. We need to be around healthy people. David understood this when he wrote Psalm 1:1, "Blessed is the man who does not walk in the counsel of the wicked or stand in the way of sinners or sit in the seat of mockers." In other words, be careful with whom you associate. One negative person can defeat twenty positive ones. It is easier for people to bring you down than for you to raise them up. As a final warning, Proverbs 12:26 reminds us that "a righteous man is cautious in friendship."

One of the most therapeutic and healing ministries is that of a friend. Modern educational institutions are beginning to understand the importance of touch. Psychology teaches that we need seven meaningful touches a day to be happy. The University of Miami School of Medicine has a "Touch Research Institute." Some of the findings of this Institute show that touch can fight depression, decrease the stress hormones the body produces, and enhance sleep. Massage can reduce the stress of business men and women who fly a lot. A couple of major airports are now offering back massages for the travelers. Research shows that after a 15-minute massage, employees are more alert and perform better on math problems. The institute director Maria Hernandez-Reif says that, "Touch is often seen as a taboo in our culture; that's only because we've forgotten our early ways. Touch is one of our earliest forms of healing. We need to get back to that." More touch means less stress and less touch means more stress (Condensed from Tom McNichols, "The Power of Touch," USA Weekend [February 6-8, 1998], p. 22).

8. *When possible get out and get some sun.* In *Harvard Health Letter*, February 1996, pp. 7-8, research shows that 10 million Americans have a condition called seasonal affective disorder (SAD). About 25 million others have a lesser degree of SAD called "winter blues." This condition is associated with a change of melatonin level in the body. Melatonin is the body's

own sleep aid. It is gradually introduced into the body at night-fall. This makes people sleepy. The days are shorter in the winter, so it is believed that there is more melatonin in the body at this time. It is believed that light triggers the body not to dump melatonin into the system.

9. *Stay away from alcohol and other drugs.* Proverbs 20:1-2 says this: "Wine is a mocker and beer a brawler; whoever is led astray by them is not wise." Proverbs 23:29-35 spells out the details:

> Who has woe? Who has sorrow? Who has strife? Who has complaints? Who has needless bruises? Who has bloodshot eyes? Those who linger over wine, who go to sample bowls of mixed wine. Do not gaze at wine when it is red, when it sparkles in the cup, when it goes down smoothly! In the end it bites like a snake and poisons like a viper. Your eyes will see strange sights and your mind imagine confusing things. You will be like one sleeping on the high seas, lying on top of the rigging. "They hit me," you will say, "but I'm not hurt! They beat me, but I don't feel it! When will I wake up so I can find another drink?"

Many people attempt to deal with stress with the use of alcohol. Alcohol does induce sleep, but the sleep cycle may be disrupted later because of the alcohol. So the drinker now has two problems. The original problem is still there, and because the sleep cycle has been affected negatively he or she has the problem of coping with sleep loss. So stress has been compounded by the use of alcohol, not aided. Some research has shown that moderate consumption of alcohol reduces the risk of cardiovascular disease. I personally believe that drinking grape juice would lower the risk without increasing other risks that drinking alcohol causes.

10. *Do things on a regular basis that make you laugh.* You might have to do things that help you learn to laugh. Laughter is one of the best medicines in the world. During times of stress, laughter is one of the first things to go! I have often heard stressed out people say, "Life is no laughing matter." Sometimes indeed life is no laughing matter, but it would be a sad commentary to live out a life with that philosophy.

In Proverbs 15:13 Solomon writes, "A happy heart makes the face cheerful, but heartache crushes the spirit." Proverbs 15:15: "All the days of the oppressed are wretched, but the cheerful heart has a continual feast." Finally, in Proverbs 17:22, "A cheerful heart is good medicine, but a crushed spirit dries up the bones." We need to spend more time laughing. It is very therapeutic and beneficial to the spirit, soul, and body of man. Chapter 7 of this book deals with laughter and stress in greater detail.

11. *Take one thing at a time.* Doing more than one thing at once makes you feel you have accomplished nothing. Solomon writes that there is a time for everything (Eccl. 3:1). Stress can be reduced when you complete one task before you start another one.

Make sure that your life has organization and that you work ahead of time to get things done. Ben Franklin said, "Dost thou love life? Then do not squander time, for that is the stuff life is made of." One important goal is not to procrastinate. Procrastination only produces more stress. Stephen Covey (author of *The 7 Habits of Highly Effective People*) said, "The key is not to prioritize what's on your schedule, but to schedule your priorities."

When you are finished with a task, throw away the materials from the task that are no longer needed. B.C. Forbes said, "Next to the dog, the wastebasket is your best friend." We have several choices when it comes to paper on our desk. Act on it immediately, file it for later reference, read it at a later time, or throw it away. One of the best ways to relax and reduce stress is to finish jobs without procrastination. Procrastination promotes and prolongs stress.

12. *Get enough rest and sleep.* Even Jesus and his disciples needed rest. Jesus told his disciples, "Come with me by your-

selves to a quiet place and get some rest" (Mark 6:31). He told them this because people were making so many demands of the disciples that they did not even have time to eat.

Paul, too, needed rest. At one point in his missionary journeys, he points out the results of lack of rest. He writes, "For when we came into Macedonia, this body of ours had no rest, but we were harassed at every turn — conflicts on the outside, fears within" (2 Cor. 7:5).

Other Scriptures refer to rest as a blessing from the Lord. Deuteronomy 33:12 gives a visual on resting in the Lord: "Let the beloved of the LORD rest secure in him, for he shields him all day long, and the one the LORD loves rests between his shoulders." David longs for rest in Psalm 55:5-6 "Fear and trembling have beset me; horror has overwhelmed me. I said, 'Oh, that I had the wings of a dove! I would fly away and be at rest.'" In Psalm 116:7 he reassures himself: "Be at rest once more, O my soul, for the LORD has been good to you."

Rest is valuable, but sleep is an essential ingredient for stress management. Much research has been done on sleep. There are two types of sleep, REM (rapid eye movement) and non-REM. Normal sleep begins with non-REM. After about 1.5 hours of sleep REM kicks in. REM is dreaming sleep; during this cycle the brain nerve cells are very active. Blood flow in the brain and muscle activity in the ear increases during REM.

REM sleep is the real deep, dreaming sleep that helps in stress management. At times alcohol and other drugs can alter the sleep pattern, possibly robbing a person of REM sleep. REM deprivation is frequently expressed in the body as impaired memory and concentration, anxiety, irritability and tiredness. Normal sleep consists of 4-6 cycles of non-REM and REM. Each cycle is about 60 to 90 minutes. REM sleep appears to be necessary for learning and memory. Non-REM appears to be necessary for feeling rested upon waking up (Modified from the Institute of Medicine, *Sleeping Pills, Insomnia and Medical Practice* [Washington, DC: National Academy of Sciences, 1979], pp. 18-20).

13. *Stop trying to be perfect — be positive and persistent instead.* One of the best ways to cure the body of stress is to heal the mind of negative thoughts. Positive beliefs are called faith and they bring peace. Solomon in Proverbs makes some astonishing remarks about thoughts. He wrote: "Above all else, guard your heart, for it is the wellspring of life." In other words, your thoughts form your life (Prov. 4:23).

"Hope deferred makes the heart sick, but a longing fulfilled is a tree of life." (Proverbs 13:12)

"For as he thinketh in his heart, so is he . . . ." (Prov. 23:7, KJV)

You're not perfect, so you will fail at this attempt. Set goals that can be reached. Luke 6:26 and Matthew 10:22 teach us that we should not set the goal to be liked by everyone.

14. *Allow yourself to cry when you need to; it is a God-given way of dealing with stress.* Jesus wept when he was distressed (Matthew 27:46,50). He wept over Lazarus (John 11:35,38). The writer of Hebrews says of Jesus, "During the days of Jesus' life on earth, he offered up prayers and petitions with loud cries and tears to the one who could save him from death, and he was heard because of his reverent submission" (Heb. 5:7).

Frequently you hear the phrase, "a sigh of relief," or "tears of relief." Actually it is tears of release — release of stress. Tears are emotional stitches for the soul. David understood this, "I am worn out groaning; all night long I flood my bed with weeping and drench my couch with tears (Ps. 6:6).

Twice in Revelation it says that God will wipe away every tear (Rev. 7:17; 21:4). What a great thought. God won't laugh at our tears, he will simply wipe them away! Isaiah 38:5 says, "Go and tell Hezekiah, 'This is what the LORD, the God of your father David, says: I have heard your prayer and seen your tears; I will add fifteen years to your life.'"

I was recently at a college basketball game in which the winner of the game became the number one seed for the conference tournament. It was a really close game with some questionable calls by the refs. When it ended Ball State had won. My wife Janelle and I both know the coach and his wife fairly well, so we went down to talk with his wife. When we got down to her, all she did was hug Janelle and cry. Janelle also started to cry. These were tears of happiness, but also of stress relief.

I can only imagine the stress that must have been on Wendy during the game. How nervous and tense she must have been as she watched the game go on. A thousand thoughts ran through her mind as the score became extremely close. When the final horn blew, the stress was over and the tears could flow.

David wrote, "Evening, morning and noon I cry out in distress, and he hears my voice (Ps. 55:17). He also wrote, "Record my lament; list my tears on your scroll — are they not in your record?" (Ps. 56:8) Psalm 126:5-6 states, "Those who sow in tears will reap with songs of joy. He who goes out weeping, carrying seeds to sow, will return with songs of joy, carrying sheaves with him."

15. *Accept what you cannot change.* Focus and change the things you can change. In other words, have a cause in which you believe. Have a dream that is worth fighting for, a vision to which you are willing to give your life! The serenity prayer of AA goes along with this concept, "God grant me the serenity to accept the things I cannot change, the courage to change the things I can, and the wisdom to know the difference."

16. *Become your best friend.* Be good to yourself. Treat yourself the same way you would treat your best friend if he or she were in the same situation.

Being loving and gentle to yourself during times of stress is a great way of coping with it. Turning on yourself and becoming your worst enemy during times of stress will only make the situation worse. People frequently tell me how hard it is for them to love themselves, but it is easy for them to hate themselves.

When Jesus was asked what the greatest command was, he gave two. Love God and love your neighbor as yourself (Matt.

22:37-40). He assumed you love yourself when he gave this command. Loving yourself gives you a great resource in dealing with stress.

17. *Realize that stress and trouble are parts of life* (Job 14:1; Ps. 90:10; John 16:33). God is still in control, and your troubles will pass. David and the other writers of Psalms frequently write about trouble.

9:9: "The LORD is a refuge for the oppressed, a stronghold in times of trouble."

10:14: "But you, O God, do see trouble and grief; you consider it to take it in hand. The victim commits himself to you; you are the helper of the fatherless."

22:11: "Do not be far from me, for trouble is near and there is no one to help."

27:5: "For in the day of trouble he will keep me safe in his dwelling; he will hide me in the shelter of his tabernacle and set me high upon a rock."

32:7: "You are my hiding place; you will protect me from trouble and surround me with songs of deliverance."

41:1-3: "Blessed is he who has regard for the weak; the LORD delivers him in times of trouble. The LORD will protect him and preserve his life; he will bless him in the land and not surrender him to the desire of his foes. The LORD will sustain him on his sickbed and restore him from his bed of illness."

46:1-2: "God is our refuge and strength, an ever-present help in trouble. Therefore we will not fear, though the earth give way and the mountains fall into the heart of the sea."

59:16: "But I will sing of your strength, in the morning I will sing of your love; for you are my fortress, my refuge in times of trouble."

86:7: "In the day of my trouble I will call to you, for you will answer me."

91:15: "He will call upon me, and I will answer him; I will be wtih him in trouble, I will deliver him and honor him."

107:6: "Then they cried out to the LORD in their trouble, and he delivered them from their distress."

116:3: "The cords of death entangled me, the anguish of the grave came upon me; I was overcome by trouble and sorrow."

119:143: "Trouble and distress have come upon me, but your commands are my delight."

138:7: "Though I walk in the midst of trouble, you preserve my life; you stretch out your hand against the anger of my foes, with your right hand you save me."

I heard a great statement the other day:

> Good morning. This is God. I will be handling all of your problems today. I will not need your help. So have a good day!
>   Love,
>   God

Stress occurs the most when we try to tackle the tasks that belong to God. We try to control the universe and the world around us when it cannot be done. This creates burnout and frustration. We need to learn to let God do what God does, and let us do what we can do. These two tasks are not the same.

18. *Don't ever go to bed with guilt, fear, or anger.* Work out these emotions before the day is over. These emotions will prevent a restful sleep. When you carry them from one day to another, they will eventually wear you down. Woody Allen in one of his movies said, "I can't express anger. I internalize it and grow a tumor instead." This may have been a joke, but this is the opposite of what you want to do. You need to make it your goal to express, not internalize, these emotional strongholds.

These emotions block the spiritual and soul airways. These emotions flatten and crush the spirit and soul. This in turn leads to the body being affected adversely. This obstruction can eventually kill, steal, and destroy life. These emotions drain and strain the human spirit, soul, and body.

Once again, it fascinates me when I realize that the book of Psalms deals openly with these emotions. These emotions need to be expressed and dealt with in a biblically correct, healthy way. Our body was not designed by God to carry these emotions internally; this is why Satan likes us to repress them.

I teach a principle called the emotional Heimlich maneuver. This is where these emotions are forced out through communication. The first step is to admit what emotion you are carrying. The second step is to understand how and why the emotion developed. The third step is knowing the reasons for expressing the emotion and the benefits when you do. The fourth step is the actual expression of the emotion. This can be done through role play, unmailed letters, or face-to-face confrontation. Your mouth needs to let your ears hear what you have been harboring in your heart, for it has been holding you back all these years.

19. *Do something for others.* Doing something for others gives you a blessing. Paul quotes Jesus as saying, "It is more blessed to give than to receive," in Acts 20:35. Proverbs 11:24-26 also deals with this concept: "One man gives freely, yet gains even more; another withholds unduly, but comes to poverty. A generous man will prosper; he who refreshes others will himself be refreshed. People curse the man who hoards grain, but blessing crowns him who is willing to sell."

Doing things for others will not only bless and refresh you, but it will also help you to get your mind off of your problems and put your problems in proper perspective. This is the right way to deal with stress.

20. *Balance work and recreation.* I like the statement, "When I works, I works hard. When I plays, I plays hard." I

believe that balance is a key discipline to overcoming stress. If one works too much, then the recreational side of life is out of balance, creating stress. Do a variety of activities you enjoy. One of the key ingredients in balance is flexibility. It is frequently being flexible – "going with the flow" – that gets rid of stress.

21. *Drink plenty of water daily.* I would encourage you to take half your weight and drink that many ounces a day. (for example if you weigh 140 pounds – drink 70 ounces of water a day.) This might seem like too much, but you will feel better doing this. Your body will adapt to this new intake. First Kings 19:6 reminds us that drinking water is necessary for good health.

22. *Eat good meals.* Remember that there are three meals to eat. That's breakfast, lunch, and dinner. Healthy snacks are also very good to eat. When you eat, watch your fat intake. I know many people who miss breakfast on a regular basis, although this is not good for your body and actually increases stress.

Nutrition is one of our God-given ways to deal with stress and enhances the immune system. One of the best ways to improve your diet is to find out how many fat grams your doctor says you should be eating daily. I am not a health food junky. I like my beef, but I do try to keep my fat count down. The American Heart Association suggests that thirty percent or less of calories come from fat (and no more than ten percent from saturated fat). The labels on food will give you this information. On a 2,200 calorie diet for an active person, this means between 220 and 660 fat calories. This would be 24-73 grams of fat.

Many people believe that most of our calories should come from whole grains, vegetables and fruits. We should eat foods that contain a lot of fiber. One of the best ways to get vegetables in your diet on a regular basis is to eat what is in season. During the winter try winter squash, sweet potatoes, yams and tomatoes. They have plenty of carotenoids and bioflavenoids that fight diseases. These phytochemicals also give vegetables and fruits their color. I was told by a dietitian that the better and brighter the color of the vegetable and fruit the better it is for you.

You should not eliminate all fat from your diet. Fat tastes good and God created it for a reason. Colleen Pierre, RD says, "You need fat in your diet for your body to absorb the fat-soluble vitamins: A, D, E and K. If you don't eat enough fat, you might become vitamin deficient and possibly develop gall disease" (Joe Weider's *Shape* magazine [September 1997], p. 101). The unsaturated fat your body needs is found in avocados, olives, nuts, canola and corn oil. Salads are a great source for all these vitamins. Dark green vegetables have high levels of Vitamins A and C and folic acid.

Isn't God wonderful? He developed food not only to nourish our bodies, but also to help them develop and deal with stress! And some people believe that our creation and the world, with all its plants and animals, were just by accident!

Dr. Ornish has come up with a heart-healthy diet that is revolutionary. It consists of only 10% of calories coming from fat. He also had his patients do moderate exercise, stop smoking and attend stress management and group support meetings. His approach has been shown to have produced a reduction in cholesterol and blood pressure. It has also been shown to reduce weight (*HealthNews* [March 25, 1997], p. 4).

The food pyramid says we should eat:

6-11 servings a day from the grain group
3-5 servings a day from the vegetable group
2-4 servings a day from the fruit group
2-3 servings a day from the milk group
2-3 servings a day from the meat group
Others (fats, sweets and oils) use sparingly.

The Bible has some insights into food and nutrition that are very similar to this pyramid. The book of Daniel states about Daniel's diet,

But Daniel resolved not to defile himself with the royal food and wine, and he asked the chief official for permission not to defile himself this way. Now God had caused the official to show favor and sympathy to Daniel, but the official told Daniel, "I am afraid of my lord the king, who has assigned your food and drink. Why should he see you looking worse than the other young men your age? The king would then have my head because of you'" (Dan. 1:8-10).

Daniel asked for a ten-day test with his diet (Dan. 1:12). "At the end of the ten days they [Daniel, Hananiah, Mishael and Azariah] looked healthier and better nourished than any of the young men who ate the royal food" (Dan. 1:15).

Nutrition is one of the best ways to deal with stress. Consider what we read in 1 Samuel 14:27-28 when Jonathan ate.

But Jonathan had not heard that his father had bound the people with the oath, so he reached out the end of the staff that was in his hand and dipped it into the honeycomb. He raised his hand to his mouth, and his eyes brightened. Then one of the soldiers told him, "Your father bound the army under a strict oath, saying, 'Cursed be any man who eats food today!' This is why the men are faint."

Jonathan said, "My father has made trouble for the country. See how my eyes brightened when I tasted a little of this honey. How much better it would have been if the men had eaten today some of the plunder they took from their enemies. Would not the slaughter of the Philistines have been even greater?"

The May 2, 1997, *New England Journal of Medicine* published the results of a study that showed that vitamin E from foods correlated to a reduced risk of heart disease over a seven-year follow-up after the study. The same was not true for vitamin E gained through supplements. Foods found to be high in E are olive oil, nuts, fortified cereals, kale, wheat germ, mangos, sweet potatoes and dried apricots.

23. *Become like a child again.* This means that you schedule time to play, and you commit to doing it. This is a great way to reduce stress. You all need to have squirt guns and use them. I believe it is never too late to have a great childhood. Jesus told his disciples, "unless you change and become like little children, you will never enter the kingdom of heaven" (Matt. 18:3). In John 1:12-13 we are told, "Yet to all who received him, to those who believed in his name, he gave the right to become children of God — children born not of natural descent, nor of human decision or a husband's will, but born of God."

I believe that many times stress is created because we are acting too adult. I know many people whom I consider to be laughter-deficient and terminally serious. Reinhold Niebuhr, a neoorthodox theologian, said, "What is funny about us is precisely that we take ourselves too seriously."

24. *Don't rehash the past with its mistakes, or dwell on the future. Live in the present.* One sign that people are worried and stressed about the future is the increase in the number of psychics. Any large city that has a "new age psychic" conference can expect a packed house. Many television commercials that advertise psychic readings will give you a half-hour free to get you hooked.

Another sign that people rehash the past is all the tranquilizers and antidepressants that are prescribed by physicians to patients. In the past several years there has been a real increase in the number of new drugs. Prozac has easily become a form of liquid sunshine.

Jesus said about this, "Therefore do not worry about tomorrow, for tomorrow will worry about itself. Each day has enough trouble of its own" (Matt. 6:34). In Isaiah 43:18 we are told, "Forget the former things; do not dwell on the past." Paul wrote, "Brothers, I do not consider myself yet to have taken hold of it. But one thing I do: Forgetting what is behind and straining toward what is ahead, I press on toward the goal to win the prize for which God has called me heavenward in Christ Jesus" (Phil. 3:13-14). You cannot change the past or control the

future, so you might as well sit back and just relax. Enjoy today
— it is a gift from God (Ps. 118:24).

Jesus said about the Holy Spirit, "But when he, the Spirit of
truth, comes, he will guide you into all truth. He will not speak
on his own; he will speak only what he hears, and he will tell
you what is yet to come" (John 16:13). God through Jeremiah
said, "'For I know the plans I have for you,' declares the LORD,
'plans to prosper you and not to harm you, plans to give you
hope and a future.'"

Part of the problem is that God does not reveal his plans to
us all at once. He reveals them to us one page at a time. This is
stressful, and it is hard to be patient. But it would be more
stressful to know the complete plans that God has for us,
because this would create panic and anxiety. We don't need to
know the plans for our future, or go to a fortune teller; all we
need to know is he who knows our future. Trusting in him and
his plans for our lives is one of the ways to get rid of stress.

25. *Stop all self-criticism.* Paul writes that no unwholesome
talk should come out of our mouths (Eph. 4:29). He also writes
that God gave him authority to build people up not to tear them
down (2 Cor. 10:8; 13:10).

Most people think that criticism motivates. This is just not
true. Self-criticism is demotivating, and it is something that
Jesus never did. He had many times he could have turned on
himself. He could have asked the question, "What's wrong with
me?" or "Why don't they believe me?"

Criticizing yourself during times of crisis and stress only
makes the matter worse. One of my goals for the people that I
work with is that they become their best friend. If you told your
best friend verbally what you have been telling yourself internally you would lose a friend.

26. *Find enjoyment in what you do.* If there are tasks at
work and home that you don't enjoy doing, sandwich them

between two things that you enjoy doing. I call this the "Oreo" method of stress management.

If you are doing a job about which you have a bad attitude, I would encourage you to ask God to change your attitude about your job. Paul wrote about what our attitude should be.

> Your attitude should be the same as that of Christ Jesus: Who, being in very nature God, did not consider equality with God something to be grasped, but made himself nothing, taking the very nature of a servant, being made in human likeness. And being found in appearance as a man, he humbled himself and became obedient to death — even death on a cross! Therefore God exalted him to the highest place and gave him the name that is above every name, that at the name of Jesus every knee should bow, in heaven and on earth and under the earth, and every tongue confess that Jesus Christ is Lord, to the glory of God the Father (Phil. 2:5-11).

Enjoying, not tolerating and putting up with, your work will help to relieve stress. God wants us to rejoice in what we put our hands to. Deuteronomy 12:7 states, "There, in the presence of the LORD your God, you and your families shall eat and shall rejoice in everything you have put your hand to, because the LORD your God has blessed you." Deuteronomy 12:18 confirms, "Instead, you are to eat them in the presence of the LORD your God at the place the LORD your God will choose — you, your sons and daughters, your menservants and maidservants, and the Levites from your towns — and you are to rejoice before the LORD your God in everything you put your hand to."

Solomon writes,

> Then I realized that it is good and proper for a man to eat and drink, and to find satisfaction in his toilsome labor under the sun during the few days of life God has given him — for this is his lot. Moreover, when God gives any man wealth and possessions, and enables him to enjoy them, this is a gift of God. He seldom reflects on the days of his life, because God keeps him occupied with gladness of heart (Eccl. 5:18-20).

God wants us to enjoy life. Jesus said in John 10:10 he wants us to have abundant life. This is a gift from God. In fact every day that you have is a gift of God. He wants us to rejoice and be glad in it (Ps. 118:24).

27. *Praise God daily.* Don't forget that God is working in your stressful situation (Deut. 8:10-20). Don't forget that God is working in your life even when you can't see him. In central Indiana during the winter we may go days without seeing the sun. The fact is that no matter how thick and dark the clouds are, the sun is still there. God is the same way. No matter how dark the situation looks and how far away you feel God is, he is right there.

One of the best times to praise God is during church on Sunday. Recent research by psychiatrist Herold Koenig from Duke University has revealed some interesting findings about church attendance. He surveyed 1,718 older adults in North Carolina. He found, "Those who go to church or synagogue regularly are physically healthier, mentally healthier and they have healthier immune systems. It certainly appears that they are healthier." He measured blood levels of IL-6, an undesirable immune system protein. He found that this protein was lower in older adults (over 65) who attended church at least weekly (From AP 10/22/97).

Praise is a wonderful way to deal with stress. Psalm 150:6 teaches, "Let everything that has breath praise the LORD. Praise the LORD." The word praise is found in the NIV translation of the Bible 340 times. Praising God for his blessings and for who he is gets rid of stress. It puts things in proper perspective. Praise puts God in the stressful picture of your life. Praise makes God bigger and your problem smaller.

One of the most popular words found in the book of Psalms is the word "praise." It is found approximately 220 times. The fact is, God deserves our praise because of what he has done for us. We should not only praise him for what he has done, but also praise him for who he is.

The phrase "Hallelu Yah" is found often in Scripture. It means "Praise the Lord." In Psalms this phrase is found in verses 111:1; 112:1; 113:1, among others.

Some of the passages in Psalms that I like the most that deal with praise are

18:3 — "I call to the LORD, who is worthy of praise, and I am saved from my enemies."

22:3 — "Yet you are enthroned as the Holy One; you are the praise of Israel." The KJV passage says, "But thou art holy, O thou that inhabitest the praises of Israel."

48:1 — "Great is the LORD, and most worthy of praise, in the city of our God, his holy mountain."

52:9 — "I will praise you forever for what you have done; in your name I will hope, for your name is good. I will praise you in the presence of your saints."

54:6 — "I will sacrifice a freewill offering to you; I will praise your name, O LORD, for it is good."

56:10-11 — "In God, whose word I praise, in the LORD, whose word I praise — in God I trust; I will not be afraid. What can man do to me?"

65:1 — "Praise awaits you, O God, in Zion; to you our vows will be fulfilled."

68:4 "Sing to God, sing praise to his name, extol him who rides on the clouds — his name is the LORD — and rejoice before him."

68:19 — "Praise be to the Lord, to God our Savior, who daily bears our burdens."

68:26 — "Praise God in the great congregation; praise the LORD in the assembly of Israel."

69:34-35 — "Let heaven and earth praise him, the seas and all that move in them, for God will save Zion and rebuild the cities of Judah."

113:3 — "From the rising of the sun to the place where it sets, the name of the LORD is to be praised."

134:1-2 — "Praise the LORD, all you servants of the LORD who minister by night in the house of the LORD. Lift up your hands in the sanctuary and praise the LORD."

135:1-3 — "Praise the LORD. Praise the name of the LORD; praise him, you servants of the LORD, you who minister in the house of the LORD, in the courts of the house of our God. Praise the LORD, for the LORD is good; sing praise to his name, for that is pleasant."

28. *Study the Bible daily;* it is the only book God wrote. Paul writes about the word of God, "Did the word of God originate with you? Or are you the only people it has reached? (1 Cor. 14:36). Reading the Bible daily is a command (Josh. 1:8). It helps you to "fix your thoughts on Jesus" (Heb. 3:1). It helps us to have perseverance as we run the race marked out for us and to help us "fix our eyes on Jesus" (Heb. 12:1-2). Don Polston writes about this, "If we gaze at Jesus and glance at evil, you can't help being an optimist. If you gaze at evil and glance at Jesus, you can't help being a pessimist." (Don Polston, *Living without Losing* [Eugene, OR: Harvest House Publishers, 1975], p. 157).

In Deuteronomy 11:18-21 God tells us to

> Fix these words of mine in your hearts and minds; tie them as symbols on your hands and bind them on your foreheads. Teach them to your children, talking about them when you sit at home and when you walk along the road, when you lie down and when you get up. Write them on the doorframes of your houses and on your gates, so that your days and the days of your children may be many in the land that the Lord swore to give your forefathers, as many as the days that the heavens are above the earth.

Paul writes,

> But as for you, continue in what you have learned and have become convinced of, because you know those from whom you

learned it, and how from infancy you have known the holy Scriptures, which are able to make you wise for salvation through faith in Christ Jesus. All Scripture is God-breathed and is useful for teaching, rebuking, correcting and training in right-eousness, so that the man of God may be thoroughly equipped for every good work (2 Tim. 3:14-17).

Jesus said, "Man does not live on bread alone, but on every word that comes from the mouth of God" (Matt. 4:4; Deut. 8:3). He also said, "Do not work for food that spoils, but for food that endures to eternal life, which the Son of Man will give you. On him God the father has placed his seal of approval" (John 6:27).

Reading a Psalm a day is a great way to get the spiritual food needed to get a grip on stress. Psalm 63:1 says it in a single verse, "O God, you are my God, earnestly I seek you; my soul thirsts for you, my body longs for you, in a dry and weary land where there is no water." By daily reading the Bible we quench our thirst. I am a big fan of "BIGO":

Bible
In
Garbage
Out

Paul writes in Colossians 3:16, "Let the word of Christ *dwell* in you *richly* as you teach and admonish one another with all wisdom, and as you sing psalms, hymns and spiritual songs with gratitude in your hearts to God." The word "dwell" means live; "richly" means abundantly. In Romans 15:4 Paul gives three major reasons for reading the Bible, "For everything that was written in the past was written to teach us, so that through *endurance* and the *encouragement* of the Scriptures we might have *hope*." These are three fruits of reading the Bible. This includes the Old Testament as well as the new.

29. *Dwell on God's promises.* God's promises give us hope for the future in times of stress. Paul writes that all of God's promises have "yes" for an answer (2 Cor. 1:20-21). First John

4:4 is one of my favorite promises in the Bible, "greater is he that is in you, than he that is in the world" (KJV).

One of God's greatest promises is that his presence will always be with us (Ps. 139:7-10; Matt. 28:20). Another promise that brings peace in stressful times is that God's eyes and ears are attentive to our prayers (1 Pet. 3:12). God is not slow in answering his promises, even though they may not come in our time zone (2 Pet. 3:9). Psalms talks a lot about the promises of God

77:8 — "Has his unfailing love vanished forever? Has his promise failed for all time?" The answer to both of these questions is "No!"

119:41-42 — "May your unfailing love come to me, O LORD, your salvation according to your promise; then I will answer the one who taunts me, for I trust in your word."

119:50 — "My comfort in my suffering is this: Your promise preserves my life."

119:58 — "I have sought your face with all my heart; be gracious to me according to your promise."

119:162 — "I rejoice in your promise like one who finds great spoil."

The writer of Hebrews says about God's promises,

When God made his promise to Abraham, since there was no one greater for him to swear by, he swore by himself, saying, "I will surely bless you and give you many descendants." And so after waiting patiently, Abraham received what was promised.

Men swear by someone greater than themselves, and the oath confirms what is said and puts an end to all argument. Because God wanted to make the unchanging nature of his purpose very clear to the heirs of what was promised, he confirmed it with an oath. God did this so that, by two unchangeable things in which it is impossible for God to lie, we who have fled to take hold of the hope offered to us may be greatly encouraged. We have this hope as an anchor for the soul, firm and secure. It enters the inner sanctuary behind the curtain, where Jesus, who went before us, has entered on our behalf. He has become a high priest forever, in the order of Melchizedek (6:13-20).

30. *Learn to be still, wait patiently, and trust God.* The writer of Hebrews states, "We do not want you to become lazy, but to imitate those who through faith and patience inherit what has been promised" (Heb. 6:12). Zechariah 2:13 commands, "Be still before the Lord, all mankind, because he has roused himself from his holy dwelling." Habakkuk 2:20 declares, "But the Lord is in his holy temple; let all the earth be silent before him." By trusting God and being still, this means that we do not become self-reliant.

Self-reliance is guaranteed to produce burnout and stress because:

    a. You feel that you have to do it all. That you have to make all the decisions.

    b. You realize that you can't do everything you need to do, so this becomes overwhelming.

    c. You begin to believe that failure is only a matter of time. This causes you to fret.

Being still, waiting patiently, and trusting God are three very difficult things to do, but all three create spiritual health. In Psalms this concept is frequently taught

21:7 — "For the king trusts in the Lord; through the unfailing love of the Most High he will not be shaken."

22:8 — "He trusts in the Lord; let the Lord rescue him. Let him deliver him, since he delights in him." This verse was a mocking by David's enemies. They knew David trusted God and they tried to make an insult out of this trust.

27:14 — "Wait for the Lord; be strong and take heart and wait for the Lord."

28:7 — "The Lord is my strength and my shield; my heart trusts in him, and I am helped. My heart leaps for joy and I will give thanks to him in song."

32:10 — "Many are the woes of the wicked, but the Lord's unfailing love surrounds the man who trusts in him."

37:7 — "Be still before the LORD and wait patiently for him; do not fret when men succeed in their ways, when they carry out their wicked schemes."

40:1 — "I waited patiently for the LORD, he turned to me and heard my cry."

46:10 — "'Be still, and know that I am God; I will be exalted among the nations, I will be exalted in the earth.'"

56:3 — "When I am afraid, I will trust in you."

56:11 — "In God I trust; I will not be afraid. What can man do to me?"

84:12 — "O LORD Almighty, blessed is the man who trusts in you."

31. *Pour out your heart to God in prayer* (Ps. 62:8). Prayer with tears is a way of emptying yourself of stress. Praying should be done on a regular basis (1 Thess. 5:17). David writes, "Evening, morning and noon I cry out in distress, and he hears my voice" (Ps. 55:17). These are the best times to pray to God and also read the Bible.

I picture prayer as a way of pouring my stressor out to God and over God. David writes, "I cry aloud to the LORD; I lift up my voice to the LORD for mercy. I pour out my complaint before him, before him I tell my trouble" (Ps. 142:1-2). Prayer is the process of surrendering problems to God. It is a way of giving God our concerns and making them his.

Prayer is me giving him my stressor and pain and him giving me peace in its place. We are instructed to cast all of our cares and stressors on Jesus (1 Pet. 5:7). My greatest prayer in times of distress is Peter's prayer to Jesus while he was walking on the water. Peter cried out, "Lord, save me" (Matt. 14:30). This is a powerful three word prayer.

Some prayers in distress are found in Psalms:

4:1 — "Answer me when I call to you, O my righteous God. Give me relief from my distress; be merciful to me and hear my prayer."

18:6 — "In my distress I called to the LORD; I cried to my God for help. From his temple he heard my voice; my cry came before him, into his ears."

118:5-7 — "In my anguish I cried to the LORD, and he answered me by setting me free. The LORD is with me; I will not be afraid. What can man do to me? The LORD is with me; he is my helper. I will look in triumph on my enemies."

120:1 — "I call on the LORD in my distress, and he answers me."

In each of the above verses, not only is the psalmist praying in distress, but he writes that the Lord answers his prayers. What a great idea to bring peace in stressful times!

It is in the times that we pour our hearts out to God that He draws near us (Jas. 4:8). This is because by prayer we draw closer to God. He wants us to tell him what we are thinking, and feeling. Even though he knows these things he would like us to tell him what we are going through. It is very true that Jesus cares for us. Isaiah 30:19 teaches that God is gracious when we call out for help.

Not only would I suggest you pray to God, but I would also have you ask people to pray about the things that are concerning you. Allow others to carry your burden by prayer (Gal. 6:2). Knowing that people are praying for you is a great way to decrease stress.

When you ask people to pray for you, don't compare your prayer request with the requests of others. Don't think that your concerns are small and insignificant compared to others'. Don't minimize your prayer needs by thinking others have more urgent needs to be dealt with in prayer than you do. All prayers are important to God.

As I close this book, I want to give you an acrostic on dealing with stress.

> **S**eek God and give him your problems (Ps. 34:4; Jas. 4:8; 2 Chr. 26:5).
>
> **T**rust him; he is our fortress (Ps. 46:7,11).
>
> **R**ely on God for your strength (Ps. 18:1).
>
> **E**njoy the presence of God in your life (Ps. 89:15; 139:7-9). He is so good to us (Nahum 1:7).
>
> **S**ee the positives and potentials in your life (Phil. 4:8).
>
> **S**ense how much God loves you (John 3:16).

SELECTED BIBLIOGRAPHY

Braun, Jay, and Darwyn E. Linder. *Psychology Today.* New York: Random House, 1979.

DeKok, Joy. "Infertility — the Death of a Dream." *Decision.* (November 1997), pp. 14-15.

"Differences among women in how they handle stress." *The Evening Press.* Muncie, IN: December 31, 1994.

Holmes, Thomas H., and Richard H. Rahe. "The Social Readjustment Rating Scale." *Journal of Psychosomatic Research.* (1967): 213-218.

Kleinmuntz, Benjamin. *Essentials of Abnormal Psychology.* New York: Harper and Row, 1974.

Kuljula, Urho M., M.D., et al. Relationship of Leisure-time Physical Activity and Morality." *The Journal of the American Medical Association* (February 18, 1998): 440-444.

McGhee, Paul E. *Health, Healing and the Amuse System.* Dubuque, IA: Kendall/Hunt Publishing, 1996.

Menninger, Karl, M.D. *The Vital Balance.* New York: The Viking Press, 1963.

New England Journal of Medicine. May 2, 1997.

Oates, Wayne E. *Nurturing Silence in a Noisy Heart.* Garden City, NY: Doubleday, 1979.

Oliver, Gary J., Ph.D., and H. Norman Wright. *Good Women Get Angry.* Ann Arbor, MI: Servant Publications, 1995.

Patrick, Maxine L., R.N., Dr. P.H., et al. *Medical-Surgical Nursing.* Philadephia: J.B. Lippincott, 1986.

Polston, Don. *Living without Losing.* Eugene, OR: Harvest House Publishers, 1975.

Sanders, J. Oswald. *Facing Loneliness.* Grand Rapids: Discovery House, 1990.

Seid, Roberta Pollack, Ph.D. "Heartbreak Hotel." Joe Weider's *Shape* magazine, (September 1997).

Selye, Hans, and Laurence Cherry. "On the Real Benefits of Eustress." *Psychology Today.* (March 1978): 60-63, 69-70.

Siegel, Bernie S., M.D. *Peace, Love and Healing.* New York: Harper and Row, 1989.

Simonton, O. Carl, M.D., Stephanie Matthews-Simonton, and James L. Creighton. *Getting Well Again.* New York: Bantam Books, 1980.

Tabor's Cyclopedic Medical Dictionary. 17th Ed. Philadelphia: F.A. David Company, 1989.

About the Author

Charles Gerber, MA is the founder and executive director of Christian Counseling Services in Muncie, Indiana. He has authored two previous books published by College Press and is a popular national speaker.

Charley is the Stress Management Educator for Ball Memorial Hospital in Muncie and has taught classes for the Cardiac Rehabilitation Program since 1993. He has also taught these classes at several other hospitals in central Indiana.

Charley lives in Muncie with his wife, Janelee, and his two children, Joshua and Caitlyn. He is a deacon at University Christian Church in Muncie, IN.

Contact Information

Christian Counseling Services
1804 North Wheeling Ave.
Muncie, Indiana 47303

(765) 289-1631

email: CCSCharley@aol.com